Putting Wisdom to Work

Practical Mindfulness for Maximal Living 2nd Ed

★★★★★ "This book shows you how to get the best out of yourself and everyone you meet" Brian Tracy, Author of 45 books & International Success Consultant

★★★★★ Putting Wisdom to Work got me thinking of new ways to mindfully explore and enjoy life. I recommend it to anybody who wants to build awareness, acceptance and gratitude in order to live life to the fullest.
~ Laura Davis, author of The Courage to Heal and founder of The Writer's Journey

★★★★★ This book is fun. I found it practical, grounded in humor, and a refreshing, inspiring read. A great way to start the new year with purpose, hope, and a new set of realistic goals. ~Claudia B.

★★★★ A joy to read, and self-helpful too! It's an extremely well-written, charming, and effective read. Would recommend it to anyone! ~Cormac O.

★★★★ Entertaining and useful. The author does a nice job at conveying wisdom in practical terms that you can relate to your own life. Entertaining writing as well, with funny life stories! ~Dana F.

★★★★★ There are so many great "a ha" moments in this book. It hit home with a simple, yet deep, step by step organized path I could actually follow. I was inspired and received some practical answers and exercises to implement, which gave me personal power and peace of mind. ~Dhyana Kimie

★★★★★ Putting policies to work! Fun, interesting and helpful read. It covers personal growth in a refreshing way I highly recommend this book for those that are already on the path and beginners as well! ~ Wendy C.

★★★★★ Many useful insights and methods for approaching your own life in a way to maximize happiness and personal potential. ~ Harlee B.

"Life is like riding a bicycle. To keep your balance you must keep moving."

~Albert Einstein

Made in the United States of America

Renaissance Publishing

Second Edition, version 1.1 2019

ASIN: B019T3AMNI

ISBN 978-0-692-77466-3

10 9 8 7 6 5 4 3 2

~~~

This book is dedicated to everyone
who wants to embrace and fully enjoy a meaningful life
while helping others do the same.

~~~

Preface to the second edition: When I set out to write this book, my intention was to create something new and practical that helped people feel great. It's been fantastic connecting with others over our shared interest in exploring consciousness. I've come to realize that we are all wizards with the ability to change reality for ourselves and others. Sometimes we just need a little help figuring out what's next and how to go about living our dreams. Seeking wisdom has been a path to feeling focused, more personal peace and empowerment. I'm better able to manage ambitions, emotions and relationships. Practicing the techniques in the book has helped me listen better, be more effective, generous, accepting, forgiving, compassionate, expressive, confident, grateful, at ease & less bothered by outside forces. I've felt the benefits of putting the mindfulness 'rubber to the road' and am ready for more. After several interviews and presenting workshops on this material, I discovered some holes regarding topics readers felt were important to them. In addition, after practicing the activities for over a year I've been able to further fine-tune the process of progress. This second edition offers a smoother and more complete reading experience, along with additional insight to the mechanics of our marvelous minds. Once again, I submit my best effort in service to others.
~Namaste, Jeff. January 2019, Santa Cruz, CA

Putting Wisdom to Work

Practical Mindfulness for Maximal Living

Table of Contents

Up Front — **1**

1. A Look in the Mirror — **3**
≈ *Who Are You?* — *6*
≈ *Lighting Up the Mind's Eye* — *8*
≈ *Creating Meaning* — *12*
≈ *Win the Rat Race* — *18*
≈ *The True-You* — *21*
≈ *Embrace your Inner Fan* — *24*
≈ *Understanding Needs* — *29*
≈ *The Reality Zone* — *33*
≈ *The Personal Policy Institute (PPI)* — *40*

2. Five Pillars — **41**
> *Activity: Policy Pillar Report Card (PPRC)* — *43*
≈ *The Health Pillar* — *44*
≈ *The Relationships Pillar* — *47*
≈ *The Resources Pillar* — *53*
≈ *The Responsibility Pillar* — *56*
≈ *The Creativity Pillar* — *58*
> *Activity: Journey Journal* — *64*

3. Dreams with Deadlines — **67**
≈ *BeSMART Goals* — *69*
≈ *Beyond Goals to Policy* — *72*
≈ *Making Policy Personal* — *74*
≈ *Benefits of Personal Policies* — *78*
≈ *Developing Personal Policies* — *81*
> *Activity: Build a Win-List* — *83*
≈ *Coach U* — *87*
≈ *Be a Genius* — *90*

4. Master of the Universe **92**
 ≈ *The Unified Field* *93*
 ≈ *Brain Operating System (B.OS)* *96*
 ≈ *Cleaning the Lens* *100*
 ≈ *Trust Natural Intuition* *102*
 ≈ *Tapping Inner Wisdom* *104*
 ≈ *Strategic Retreat* *107*
 ≈ *Just Breathe* *109*
 ≈ *Mind Your Mantra* *113*
 > *Activity: Affirmations for Transformation* *117*
 ≈ *Get Lucky* *120*

5. Be Here Now **122**
 ≈ *Emotions as Signals* *124*
 ≈ *Develop Healthy Ego Filters* *128*
 ≈ *Practice Gratitude* *133*
 > *Activity: EasyG Jar* *137*
 >*Activity: Gratitude Garden Attitude Adjuster* *137*
 ≈ *Friend Fear* *138*
 ≈ *Peace of Mind* *139*
 ≈ *Change Agent* *142*
 ≈ *Carrots* *144*
 Appendix: Ulysses Contract & the Future You *146*
 Getting Started Making Contracts *149*
 > *Activity: Make a Ulysses Contract* *152*
 Acknowledgements *156*
 About the author *157*

Up Front

Have you ever felt there must be more to life but not sure how to grab it? Have you noticed it is impossible to think your way to inner peace? Are you ready to break free of dusty old beliefs and build a practice to release your inner wizard? Do you want a more direct path to empowered fulfillment? We all share these desires.

The good news is that it's time to relax. You are enough. The self-acceptance we seek is not about accomplishment, grand gestures or our heroic struggles. It's about relaxing into the best version of you while continuing to grow as a person. "Putting Wisdom to Work" is about learning what works while defining your own measures of success. It's about the gentle process of using acceptance to let go of resistance.

Inside you'll find practical ideas on identity, community, purpose and fun. See how mindfulness, spirituality, compassion and wisdom are the same thing. Learn how to zero in on true needs then take action to fill them. Develop wisdom skills and you'll make twice the personal growth progress in half the time!

The personal policy approach challenges you to change the things you can and stop worrying about the things you can't. See how to save time and energy by learning from the experiences of others. This is a practical guide to living your best life. Accepting wisdom as a path to peace has been my wizard's wand and it can be yours too. If you want to feel better now, get stuff done and have more fun then this book is for you. ~~~

Wisdom delivers the ability to recognize truth without proof. It shifts your perspective to meet any situation head on with clarity, purpose and love. These simple straightforward self-discovery strategies help you to be present while mindfully painting the future. Use them to unleash the law of attraction in every aspect of living. Put wisdom to work and be able to:

- Find answers to life questions.
- Shape beliefs that bend reality to avoid regrets.
- Use acceptance to let go of resistance.
- Map a more direct path to personal fulfillment.

See how to corral stress by managing self-talk beyond mindlessly grasping, rejecting, planning, remembering, worrying, and fantasizing. Get great at practicing gratitude, friending fear, and releasing inner-fan genius. Close the gap between dreams and reality by shaping personal policies for health, relationships, resources, responsibility, and creativity.

Why work on enjoying life? Because it goes by so damn fast. The days may seem long but the years are short. It's easy to get seduced by ego, feel lonely, be stuck in old ways, get trapped inside the mind, feel swept up in desire, and miss all the fun. It's also easy to decide to step back and enjoy living the life that wants to live you.

~~~ This book started around a campfire high in the Sierra Nevada Mountains. After a long day of backpacking, we gathered and quickly realized that nobody had brought anything to drink: we all thought somebody else had packed the cocktails! So instead of having a lively party, we relaxed and told stories. I shared a few instances of crazy catastrophes and mindless mayhem. Toward the end of the evening my friends all said, "*Jeff, you have to write that stuff down.*" This got me going on what has turned into a ten-year odyssey of ideas.

Though my stories were entertaining, they were no novel. As I reflected on "*mistakes*" made, the purpose of this book evolved. What started as a memoir morphed into a personal journey on how to learn from challenges, make transitions, and redefine a life in progress. Those notes grew into focusing on the balancing act of addressing obligations and enjoying life while making it all meaningful.

Writing this book has led me from disillusioned victim to grateful warrior. It is the fruit of one person's search for guiding principles and methods for creating meaning, passion, and purpose. It's how I learned to transform experience, hopes, needs, and desires into smart plans with manageable steps.

Meaning, purpose and happiness are the prizes of the process. Defining personal policies is a path to putting wisdom to work. It is a skill that can be integrated at any stage of life, situation, background, goals, religion or faith. Use practical mindfulness to relax into making the most of living while helping others do the same. Let's take the journey together.

Wisewords: *"The secret of getting ahead is getting started."* ~Mark Twain

1. A Look in the Mirror

What did the philosopher Socrates mean when he said, "the unexamined life is not worth living?" I think what he was trying to say is that those who don't update beliefs and realign needs as life unfolds can get stuck living a stale, unfulfilled existence.

Following lifestyle scripts about home, school, work, relationships and recreation can be pleasant, but may not be truly satisfying. It all depends on how you feel inside. Needs change as life evolves. If it feels like something is missing, you can bet it probably is.

The challenge is how to spot transitions, figure out what true current needs are, and (this is key) take ownership of your beliefs and expectations about the way life works. This kind of self-examination takes work. But Socrates believed this is the burden of being free, and the only way to live.

Life passages can be hard; it sometimes feels like the world is out to get you. It can also be joyful. It's a choice, a matter of perspective. There is life how we want it to be, and life as it is. The more we cling to expectations and desire, the more we struggle. Most of these scripts run unconsciously in the background. When these are negative or out of alignment with reality, you have two choices: change your expectations or change your reality. This book offers approaches to doing both.

~~~

I used to believe that hard work and persistence would bring happiness. My left-brain orientation was good at gathering degrees and material things, but I was not generally happy. I worked longer, thought harder, but forgot how to feel.

In 2008 the universe slapped me upside the head. Decades of chasing love and money sputtered out with another broken heart and stock-market crash. I woke up and realized that my hopes and expectations were not lining up with reality. I was feeling anxious and disillusioned, knew I needed to make some changes, but didn't know what to do or where to turn. I had tried many approaches, but realized most were rationalizations or coping tricks masking the real issues.

The problem was I couldn't figure out what changes my heart really desired. I had been chasing security by blindly striving and randomly savoring for a long time, but felt lost.

Sure I had some wild memories, but most of those were only useful in learning what not to do. I had landed a few good jobs, but at the end of the day the work itself was not terribly satisfying. I had enjoyed some wonderful relationships, but people change and I had to accept that peace of mind can only come from within.

There is no way to control much of what happens in life, but there are ways to transform the experience of them. I knew there was a better way. Surrendering to the wisdom of acceptance and hopeful trust fueled a path of discovery.

I dug into researching everything I could find on human nature and psychology. We are amazing creatures born with the capacity to be joyful, depressed, and everything in between. Curiosity, compassion, love, appreciation, playfulness, selflessness, and kindness are as real as self-absorption, lust, hate, violence, greed, jealousy, secretiveness, contempt, disgust, manipulation, and anger. It's all hardwired in. Add in some marketing, politics, social media and all the stress of modern living to confuse our perception of reality.

I've come to realize that experiencing challenges and longing for a happier existence does not mean that we are broken, it just comes with the duality of existence. The game is rigged to keep us striving. Comfort leads to discomfort then back. The only constant is change.

So if change is constant and going with the flow was not taking me where I wanted, I had to figure out how to intentionally change course. The practical challenges became how to raise self-awareness, what needs to focus on, and how to be patient long enough to let good stuff happen.

~~~

I started asking the big questions; what is purpose and the meaning of life? I asked, what are the areas that matter that I actually have some influence over? The five aspects that came up were healthful living (mind and body), relationships (social engagement), resources (including financial security), responsibility (to be needed), and creativity (which included fun). I felt that if these pillars were in order, the rest would fall into place. With this I started doodling on a yellow pad and saw that under each pillar were some obvious ideas for making life upgrades; I decided to call these personal policies.

Policies have helped me to exercise more regularly, cut way back on TV, read more novels, learn to sail, start a garden, meditate, become more grateful, and so much more. These thought tools have brought hope, optimism, and more feeling of meaningful existence. I had wanted these things for a long time, but it took introspection, practice and patience to map a path forward.

Our circumstances and needs may be different but we tend to ask ourselves the same basic questions. What really matters? What can we do to create and re-create the best life experience possible? The question becomes are you ready to do what it takes to wake up and live fully? What do you think is stopping you?

This book is for those who want ideas, tools, and techniques for making and keeping a great life reflection for themselves and the people around them. It explores how to keep beliefs fluid while staying present, being patient, paying attention, asking for guidance, taking action where needed, focusing on what comes next, then relaxing and enjoying the ride. Consider it a missing class from school and roadmap to defining personal success.

Whatever life transitions demand - whether it's getting fit, building more satisfying relationships, sparking romance, securing fulfilling work, learning how to relax, making time for travel - you owe it to yourself to find out who you are. With awareness of yourself and others, life upgrades are within reach. If you are ready to do the work, the rewards are yours to reap.

When you go beyond dreaming to doing, good things happen. In the chapters that follow, see how to put personal wisdom to work to carve out a piece of paradise. Let awareness, purpose, and passion drive ambitions, actions, and attitude. When doing your honest best, you'll have less regrets and become a generally happy person. The world becomes your playground, and a better place for everyone. Good deal, right? Let's get started.

Wisewords: *"Winners make a habit of manufacturing their own positive expectations in advance of the event."* ~Brian Tracy

≈ Who Are You?

Why are we so hard on ourselves? Unrealistic expectations about how life should be can really mess with your mind. Expectations pollute perception and appreciation of the imperfect present. As it turns out, I've discovered that when expectations and reality fall out of alignment, it is not failure but simply a sign that something needs to change.

Personal identity and sense of self typically come from our roles as student, worker, family, fun lover, status, etc. Nearly every identity we assume comes with established expectations, schedules and responsibilities.

As we age through life-stage identities our roles becomes less clear. Defining the self is a moving target with serious risks if one misses their cues. Changing work and family responsibilities presents challenges to feeling vital and connected. A lot of depression and health issues can be traced to loss of feeling needed, engagement and direction.

It takes awareness to know when to leave home, to focus on schooling, to work hard, to build a family or tribe, when to check off bucket list items and how to *"retire"* with a sense of purpose and meaning. Some lucky souls are blessed to be engaged with ongoing stimulating work or family life, some are not. An awful lot of retirees quickly run out of projects and travel destinations, ending up stuck in front of the TV.

Each stage of life redefines the past ones. Our sense of identity reflects whatever is currently going on. A great past (success, fame, work, family, etc.) will not guarantee a happy present. It is the current activates, connections, and interests that drive our sense of self, purpose, meaning and well-being. Past accomplishments can help us stay grateful, but fade into memory quickly. The future is just an idea. It may be hard to stay present and constantly reinvent what it means to take ownership of creating a satisfying reality, but that's life. Happiness lives in the here and now.

Like everyone, I've experienced my share of challenges: Work that felt meaningless, relationships that fizzled, financial confusion, spiritual questioning, stress, health issues, self-doubt, the list goes on. I'm generally an upbeat person, don't look for problems and don't like to dwell on difficulties, but questions kept coming up. I work hard, shouldn't I feel more engaged and have more sense of purpose? Shouldn't life be more fun?

I was tired of trying to live with the unrealistic expectations I had set for myself and placed on others. I wanted to be done with worry and power struggles, but didn't know where to turn. After spending years exploring science, spirituality, psychology, personal growth and more, the answers remained elusive. Could fulfillment be found in family? A new career? Living a life of adventure? Practicing more creativity? I had tried all of these things and still felt a longing inside. I dabbled in Zen, self-help, religion, drugs and more, never quite finding a solution that felt right. So I kept digging.

I've spent time looking for answers in church, on yoga mats, in foreign lands, and in the pages of my journals. It has all been good adventure, but still found myself seeking a more direct path to happiness, fulfillment and peace of mind. I needed a strategy to tie life experiences together in a meaningful way and help make my way through the transitions.

In my search for meaning it became clear that I had spent a lot of life waiting for dreams to somehow magically happen. I grew up feeling entitled to a happy life, good relationships, romance, financial success, and excitement. Life pleasantly slipped by as I went along with the situations and people that found me. Going with the flow seemed like a good policy. But going with the flow never pushed anyone to discover their gifts or how to share and express them.

Though I've accepted that the final answer to the meaning of life may be unknowable, there are some clues to be found. Nearly every approach to mindfulness finds that how you see the world defines how you feel about yourself in it. What you see is what you get. The world is in your mind. Creating new dimensions of life meaning is an inside job. Changing the way you see the world changes your place in it. As obvious as it sounds, this means there are exciting benefits waiting for anyone willing to let go of certainty and relax into reality.

Wisewords: *"We're all bozos on the bus, so might as well sit back and enjoy the ride."* ~Wavy Gravy

≈ Lighting Up the Mind's Eye

In Zen Buddhism there is a concept known as *Shoshin* meaning *"beginner's mind."* It refers to having an attitude of openness, eagerness, and lack of preconceptions when studying a subject, even when studying at an advanced level, just as a beginner would. Beginners do the research, ask for answers, pull on threads, and steadily go forward expecting the best.

To become a beginner, any time you look at something, anything, anyone, and begin to judge or label it, try to stop to remember that you are missing ninety percent of what's going on! Knowing there is far more going on than meets the eye is humbling. There is wisdom in uncertainty, knowing nothing is as it appears and letting go of trying to control others. Certainty is actually quite boring; where is the excitement in knowing what will happen?

A closed mind thinks only of itself and creates stress by dwelling on worries. An open mind lets go of worries and focuses on filling needs while supporting others in filling their needs. When you figure out how to cut stress and stop making decisions based on fear, things start to work out exactly as they are supposed to. Trust that everything is perfect as it is then relax into the process of walking your path.

One way to visualize the big picture of the known and unknown is visualize an eye. Every eye is made up of three circles. The small inner circle, the pupil, is what you know to be true along with an inkling of what you know you don't know. This is the knowledge you trust and live by. Even here there is a high probability that what you think you know is wrong or incomplete.

The next circle, the colored iris, is a little bigger and represents what you sort of know or understand. Things you have been exposed to but not much study or experience with. This is the danger zone where ego can overestimate abilities and pull you way off course. It's the sweet spot for finding personal policies.

Sharpening a sense of awareness is the secret weapon. It's like when thinking of buying a specific model of car, all of a sudden you see them everywhere. When you tune up awareness to notice opportunities to find solutions, be grateful, empathetic, and helpful that's what starts to show up because they are already there.

The last circle, the white sclera, is our collective consciousness. It is all the wisdom and knowledge in the universe that you are not (yet) aware of. This is the exciting juicy new stuff, missing pieces, new people, new places, new positions and possibilities calling to consciousness. Gateway parts of the you yet to be.

The skill is to open up your mind's eye to this vast well of what you don't yet know even exists, possibility, hidden potential, wisdom, surprises, all just waiting to be called in.

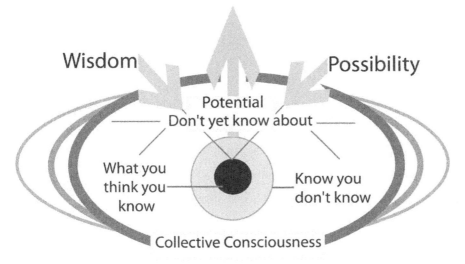

Answers live in the white space, questions waiting to be asked. Never before in history have there been so many opportunities to find answers, explore and connect. Passion lives on the path to the future. Trust intuition, take wise chances, connect with others and stay open to answers showing up just as they are needed.

~~~

Consciousness is the concept. The dictionary definition offers a good start: The state of being awake and aware of one's surroundings. Awareness by the mind of itself and the world. A little more digging reveals that personal consciousness is a bit more than paying attention; it defines who you are and fills in expectations of what is possible. Consciousness is that which makes experience possible. It's the level of awareness and personal experience within reality as we know it, and beyond. It's not that consciousness lets you see reality, consciousness is reality based on awareness and expectations.

While studying the art of conscious intention, the topic of placebo effect often comes up. In one mind-bending study at Harvard it was shown that placebo drugs had an effect on patients even after they were told the medicine was fake! The patients' accumulated conscious and unconscious expectations of doctors and medicine triggered healing on a quantum level.

Consciousness is something to participate in, draw from, and contribute to. . It is an expandable state of mind and connective energy starting with the "I" self, others, all the material and spiritual universe. The universe is consciousness.

The lower reptilian mind focuses on survival, success, pleasure, etc. The higher neocortex conscious mind is open to empathy, spirituality, and connection with others.

Raising consciousness helps to let go of ego-based thoughts, self-justification, and pride to welcome a more universal self. Higher conscious awareness works beyond self-interest, fear, and aggression in a more loving state of being. Status and material wealth fade as connection, compassion and kindness take over.

Every path to personal growth leads down the road of conscious awareness. This fleeting feeling is not something that can be possessed. It is a shared awareness only existing while we are contributing. Some of the layers of collective conscious awareness include:

- Self
- Religion, Spirituality
- Lover, Family, and Friends
- Tribe, Team, Company, Hobbies, and School
- Events, Activities, City, State, and Nation
- Plants, Animals, Rocks, Trees, Bugs, Planet, and the Universe, etc...

Maximal living is the mindful embrace of a unique awareness within the larger whole of conscious creation. The more higher consciousness is embraced the more wisdom becomes available to draw from and employ.

One example of expanding consciousness was after college. I had moved to a new town and was feeling stuck. With a fresh degree and plenty of ambition the River City had provided work and a place to live, but not community. The few friendships that came my way felt superficial. Work alone was not enough and I found myself dreading empty weekends.

One morning while jogging around the park I noticed a group of strangers playing some sort of game with a Frisbee. As I watched it seemed like they were having so much fun, running became a slow shuffle as I stared. Not knowing any of the people or the game there was no thought of asking to join in, I passed by.

Coming around the field again I slowed and stared so intensely I almost missed the gal waving me in. Conscious awareness had been sparked. Somehow curiosity overruled shyness as I wandered over to play. As it turned out the game was Ultimate and rules were easy; run, stop, and pass the disk toward the goal.

Not knowing the players and rules was challenging but in I went. Ten minutes later a leg muscle pulled painfully dropping me on the sidelines, but I was hooked. Sunday afternoons were reserved for play. Often the games rolled into an early evening barbeque where faces turned to names and relationships were born. To this day I still enjoy the game and can trace some of my best friends to that field. In trying something new I found a simple passion I am so grateful for.

Looking back I can't imagine my life in Sacramento without the people I met in those games. We have done so much together off the field. Even though I have moved away, the relationships continue to grow. Opening consciousness up to something new really paid off.

Personal experience has proven everything I'll ever need is just around the corner. The people, ideas, and answers are out there waiting to be called in. Just as an empty room echoes all sounds an open mind is available to new ideas. Making important decisions is always a gamble. By staying awake the wisdom and people that make the odds better always show up.

Next time you feel ego resistance to try something or meet someone you are curious about consider that a sign that you must go there, and prepare to be pleasantly surprised.

Wisewords: " *Life is a culmination of the past, an awareness of the present, an indication of a future beyond knowledge, the quality that gives a touch of divinity to matter.* " ~Charles Lindbergh

≈ Creating Meaning

If there is one concept to get from this book it is that YOU give everything you see all of its meaning. Love, hate, joy, sadness, excitement, and boredom. Thoughts and feelings drive the experience of reality in the mind. Think back and remember how many times your whole attitude shifted with receiving one missing piece of information. Creating meaning is about learning to focus on supportive wisdom. At any given moment you are only one thought away from peace.

Some people who have nothing are happy; some people who have everything are troubled. True wealth comes with the perspective of knowing how to relax into reality whatever it is. We put so much energy into our work, family and play but often forget that there is no separation within. Perspective reminds us that purpose is not all about changing the world, it's as much about loving it as it is. When the underlying kind mind operating system is working properly all aspects of life become one poem.

Purpose, meaning, and your mission are not something you find or possess; it's more about feeling and feeding what is already there. It's about focusing on what is well and right gratefully through self-aware living.

The source of your experience is you. Either you are paying attention (surrender+awareness+compassion) or ignoring it (attachment+mindlessness) in the present moment. Paying attention helps to embrace life at ease with reality.

We use the word reflection to describe both a mirror and the process of becoming self-aware. Enjoying life is like looking into a mirror with no edges. Maybe you like what we see, maybe you don't, but there's no use arguing with the reflection. It is what it is. Wherever you are at, whatever you are doing, there are going to be issues that get in your way of enjoying life. It's all about how you deal with it.

To enjoy life means to be willing to sometimes say "*I don't know*" and mean it. Don't pretend to understand existence or get lost in the details of being busy just to stay busy. Purpose, position, and people will come and go. Be willing to enjoy the ride comfortably without a safety line or always being able to see a guiding light. Work towards what you find meaningful, but release the need to own or control anything. Kindness counts. Instead of trying to make your mark simply make your way.

Finding purpose shows up when you allow the life living within you to unfold by finding ways to share your gifts. You are connected to everything through a force deeper than can ever be known. Embracing a sense of awe in this energy opens the mind to be present beyond thinking or planning for the future.

Thinking is not a bad thing, the skill is knowing when to step back, disengage, and simply be here now. Stay present and ready to act when called on. Accept this and you have it.

~~~

The world we perceive is not so much coming at us as it is being projected from within. Heaven, hell, love, hate, beauty, relationships, status, everything is in the mind. At every moment you are the source of all that you see and feel. You are either embracing reality or struggling against it.

What you project is what you expect. As we project expectations other people reflect them back creating the illusion that reality is exactly as you think it is, when it's not. The world is fluid, it responds and reaffirms what you believe in the form of other people, intuition, synchronicities, and situations. What you give is what you get.

Without awareness, ego unconsciously projects expectations on others, and ourselves, and then uses the feedback to reinforce beliefs. We fall in love with ideas, position, people and possessions then find we are tortured by feelings of anxiety trying to protect and control them.

One of my favorite quotes about beliefs sits alone at the front of the book, "*A Course in Miracles*" by the Foundation for Inner Peace. It reads: "*Nothing real can be threatened, nothing unreal exists.*" To me this means that reality is not always (ever!) what it appears to be, don't believe everything you think.

Our minds play tricks and fool us into believing things that are not true. Beliefs can be dangerous when they stop us from experiencing, questioning and thinking critically. False or out-of-date beliefs lead to bad decisions and create a cloudy distorted view on reality.

This process of letting beliefs explain the unexplainable is human nature. Thousands of years ago people found huge bones and immediately assumed that giants must have once roamed the planet. Over time the legends of the giants became the mythology of the Titans and Greek Gods. Zeus, Apollo, Athena are among the names given to these beings with the power to fly, create and destroy.

The bones actually belonged to dinosaurs. Another example of how we make up stories then live by them as though they are truth. Mistakes such as these have affected entire cultures in the past. How are assumptions and beliefs affecting you now?

~~~

No matter who you are, life feels hard. The self-judgmental ego of the inner-critic fuels feelings of inadequacy, aloneness, and separation. These anxieties come from a misunderstanding of consciousness.

When French philosopher René Descartes said, *"I think therefore I am,"* he set off a chain of beliefs leading to rationalism, a method of understanding the world based on the use of reason as the means to attain knowledge.

But the untamable dance of consciousness functions beyond reason. The concept comes from the Latin *"conscious"* which literally means sharing knowledge or to know together. Consciousness is not a solo act. It literally means to be interdependent, connected to every living thing constantly.

Modern society creates anxiety by promoting independence. It says we should be able to do and have it all on our own terms and timing. Striving to keep up with expectations or have it all socially, sexually and materially leaves precious little time to discover, connect, relax, appreciate, savor, and enjoy life. Even in downtime it's common to feel compelled to *"do"* something entertaining or seemingly productive.

When we try to control work, family, recreation, etc. we get stressed out trying to be, see, have, and do everything. Ego tends to think it can possess or control consciousness when what you're actually looking for is to simply be more aware.

If independence feels hard or you don't like the results of letting ego drive it's time to rethink thinking. Instead of being focused on *"what's in it for me?"* look at what you are giving. Rather than expecting others to support what you want, step back with awareness, stay present, and simply be curious. In your conscious mind, with curiosity and interdependence awareness, all feelings can find freedom.

Anxiety exists to keep us motivated and out of dangerous situations, that's it. To combat false-anxiety try on the idea of averaging life experience. It goes like this: There will be highs, there will be lows, happy, sad, engaged, bored, confident, anxious. When you step back, remember and take it all into account, add everything up and divide by gratitude it equals the authentic happy average.

The experience averaging policy works by storing positive energy in the consciousness bank when it's available then calling on it when needed. When things are going good in savoring mode (relaxing, in nature, exercising, playing music, with friends, being entertained, etc,) slow down, give thanks and make a deposit to the consciousness bank.

Open up all senses to soak up the goodness. Take pictures, add notes in a journal. Let everything flow in filling the resilience batteries. As the need to strive for something comes (studying, working, taking care of obligations, etc.) connect to the grid, reach inside, and out to others, to draw on reserves.

~~~

It seems the hardest part of accepting our human nature is knowing that no matter what you do, you will want more. The ego mind banks past experiences then quickly desires something new. As you build up currency in your "*been there done that*" account, it becomes harder to find ways to make new deposits. Relationships, work, adventure, etc. easily brings excitement easily the first few times around; keeping that feeling fresh often gets harder with age.

Add to this the phenomena of time speeding up as we get older. Our brain is triggered by novel experiences that have set memory markers in time. As we pass through significant experiences (school, career, relationships), it's common to settle into a routine of work, recreation and people. The days, weeks and years blend together and literally speed up our perception of time passing.

This is how new jobs, travel, etc. delivers the excitement fix with new sights, sounds, smells, tastes, and people. But if we only chase the new stuff we may miss out on a deeper appreciation of life as it is. This has been a problem for me. After decades of searching, the search itself became the goal. I had lost track of what I was really searching for or actually needed. I had become addicted to the illusion of newness and forgot how to simply connect and appreciate what is real and happening now.

I've come to realize that chasing the illusion of love, money, adventure or status, mindlessly triggers the feeling of aliveness, but always fails to deliver lasting satisfaction. Averaging wants with needs, gratitude, and responsibility delivers the perspective needed to wake up and live beyond 'wanting' consciousness. It releases expectations while opening the mind to true needs of self and others.

With a mindful time awareness in place, the routines of living the life can be deeply appreciated. Filling the need for newness can be satisfied by intentionally growing, doing new things, and meeting new people. The chasing morphs into experiencing, savoring and enhancing. In this case, simply understanding how our brains work delivers the power to squeeze more living into life!

As we gather experience on our journey, hopes, needs, and expectations must change to keep life fresh, interesting, and meaningful. Finding meaning is not so much a search for what works but rather an exploration into managing our inner workings. We are not what we say, the clothes we wear, what we do, or even what we think. Our connection is bigger than that and has many layers.

Our job is to peel back the "*now*" reality to expose and explore new interesting dimensions. To let go of what was while embracing what is. The perfect present is available every single moment; we simply need to remember to look for and appreciate it.

Just as the purpose of the universe might simply be to expand, our purpose might simply be to find ways to connect, do what we love then love what we do. Maybe life is about becoming our best self, and then helping others do the same. Let's dig into that.

~~~

A look at the nature of existence helps the patterns become clear. All animals need others to survive. As infants we are born one hundred percent dependent on others. Without support we would perish.

The job of parenting and raising children are perfectly paired with our DNA. This may help explain why so many people point to having children and raising a family as the source of their ultimate happiness. It feeds and fills the natural desire to create, work, nurture, and socialize.

When you break it down, raising children demonstrates meaningful patterns of action to learn from. Parenting demands mindfulness, work, planning, selflessness, and the ability to compromise and make sacrifices. To feed, educate, groom, clothe, and care for offspring requires long-term focus and commitment.

Children provide feedback and reinforce our place in society. Family life is usually filled with relationships, challenges, highs and lows, all-important pieces in the human puzzle. Raising children feeds the need to be needed and connects you to another in a permanent way.

As it turns out, some of us are better at raising children than others. Some families are tighter than others. Not everyone has the opportunity to live that lifestyle. There are also plenty of fine parents out there that feel something is missing or may just need more diversity in their routine. Raising a family is one path to connecting with meaning, and a good model to learn from. But there are many paths to contentment.

We all need to be loved, feel needed, live authentically, and be part of something bigger than ourselves. If you have anything less than this going on you will feel incomplete. Consciousness collects where like minds connect. Whatever lifestyle you choose, if you are able find ways to express your talents in the service of sharing, the rest will follow.

Wisewords: *"The perfect man employs his mind as a mirror; it grasps nothing; it refuses nothing; it receives, but does not keep.' Detachment means to have neither regrets for the past nor fears for the future; to let life take its course without attempting to interfere with its movement and change, neither trying to prolong the stay of something pleasant nor to hasten the departure of things unpleasant. To do this is to move in time with life, to be in perfect accord with its changing music, and this is called Enlightenment."* ~Chung-Tzu

≈ Win the Rat Race

One of the many "*aha*" moments while writing this book came after studying the work of Dr. Bruce Alexander. In researching the reasons behind human addiction to substances and situations, Dr. Alexander found that scientific testing on rats was always done in horrible conditions. The small, overcrowded cages didn't give the animals any place to express themselves, hunt, breed, or play. He reasoned that the rodents went for morphine to escape the hellish conditions. This led to the rat park theory.

The theory breaks down like this: rats, like people, have needs. When those are not being met we seek ways to cope, distract ourselves, or numb the pain. When life is being lived in harmony with fulfilling surroundings you are able to be your natural self. When true needs are met, bad habits and self-defeating behaviors fall away.

To test this theory, Dr. Alexander and his team built a park that met the rats needs. They had lots of room to move around, good food, water, and flooring to burrow in, mate, play, and sleep comfortably. The morphine was still available, but the rats in this cage mostly ignored it. Some curious rodents did try it, but did not become addicted like their deprived brothers and sisters. This insight is comforting and inspiring. It reminds that when we focus on fulfilling actual needs, most problems go away.

But the human mind is a bit more demanding than that of a rat. Even in ideal surroundings, most of us will adjust our expectations, dwell on past pain, idealize future abstractions, substitute wants for needs, and find something to complain about, long for, or compare ourselves to. These are the ruts we get stuck in. That's human nature and will probably never change. But when these ruts cause discomfort it's worth looking into ways to live better.

When you find yourself stuck in thought resisting something or someone, instead of confronting or trying to fix it, examine the resistance as an opportunity to become present. Most of the things (external & internal) we resist, find distasteful or unpleasant, reflect undesirable aspects of our own mind.

The self-acceptance we seek is not about accomplishment, grand gestures, or our heroic struggles. It's about the gentle process of using acceptance to let go of resistance. It takes a willingness, commitment, and skills to let go of the past, let go of the future, and enjoy life here and now.

Acceptance does not mean to sit back and do nothing. It is all about learning to see things clearly, recognize when action is necessary, and when it is not.

~~~

So what does the ideal human park look like? It seems that feeling good happens when we get to live at least close to the life we are capable of, staying busy, doing mostly things we like, and getting rewarded or recognized for our efforts.

When expectations are in balance with reality, love, respect, and acceptance come naturally. Self-defeating habits and behaviors fade away. It's a state of mind where you have everything you need to survive, relax, explore, and excel.

To be clear I'm not talking about the type of acceptance that goes along with whatever comes along. Acceptance is a present-tense mindfulness that understands there may be work that needs to be done, and implies a willingness to do it happily.

One way to figure out what your park could look like is to ask yourself: What are my needs? Are they really being met? Who would be in the park with me? What would I be doing? Get a picture going in your mind and then ask, what's missing from my current life? Even a hazy vision of the future can help pinpoint the missing pieces.

Creating your park may not be easy. Expect trouble. Though meaning is in the mind, building relationships, finding fulfilling work, recreation, and ways to self-express takes ongoing dedication. But it's human nature to choose the path of least resistance, this is how marketers and pill-pushers lure us to try, buy or medicate our way to happiness. Anything short of building five strong pillars is a substitute, the only sure way forward is through the park.

The nature of our universe dictates that change will happen, galaxies spin, seasons come and go, reality evolves, nothing stays the same. Time throws us around the sun bringing different work, new relationships, and changing interests. As much as we want stability, it's an illusion. Don't freak out. Just as extreme athletes push through pain by seeing it coming, planning to persevere maps a course forward.

Visualizing life the way you want things to evolve unleashes imagination to paint a path to progress, I call this making a win-list. This list is where you can expect to find clues on understanding emotions, owning ego, practicing gratitude, friending fear, persisting, and maintaining a peaceful mind. All paths to the park. More on this later.

~~~

When I started paying attention and thinking about what my park would look like, it became blindingly clear that I had fallen into a rat hell. By subscribing to some popular beliefs I became a caged puppet hitting the button frantically hoping for more pellets. Too much precious time had been spent chasing success on society's terms. The car, the gadget, the job, traffic, the house, were eating up life. None of these things brought much joy, life ticked by.

I needed to break out of branded patterns to find work that actually let me use my skills, find more ways to help and give back to others, figure out how to really connect with people, and remember how to have authentic fun. Thankfully, when I was about to snap, I got laid off and had time to dig in to making meaning.

Creating my personal park has turned out to be an ongoing process. There are challenges and pain that comes with having the time to confront reality, but not nearly as much pain as ignoring what it would have brought. To stay sane I have had to find faith in the process.

There are some big benefits that have come from following your heart. Finding faith to rethink needs brings an empowering hope. Opening the mind to personal truth creates meaning. Keeping beliefs fluid delivers exciting possibilities to experience joy in unlikely places. Making a path to your park will get a little easier every day.

Belief clings while faith lets go. Faith creates belief in what you cannot yet see. Have faith your park will be a place where filling real needs, supporting others, and being supported, comes naturally.

Wisewords: *"I don't believe people are looking for the meaning of life as much as they are looking for the experience of being alive."* ~Joseph Campbell

≈ The True-You

Have you become comfortable with your current life but know that there could be more? Are you getting in your own way? Are you ready to put your gifts to work for yourself and others? Start by congratulating yourself for considering a policy-based approach. Just by reading this you're already moving closer, examining life, seeking meaning, making it happen.

Perhaps the most important realization that anyone can make in the quest for personal growth is that there is no one-size-fits-all program or formula. We are each on our own journey with different stories, points of view, abilities, goals, needs, and priorities. It is good to read books, take seminars, go to school, try spiritual paths, but each can only deliver pieces to your puzzle. You are the one who has to put it all together.

The idea of a true-you builds upon wisdom in the Delphic maxim and motto "*know thyself*" popularized by Plato, Socrates and others. These fellows understood that only you can figure out what your unique true needs are and that as we gain knowledge of ourselves we find understanding of others beyond comparison.

Comparing yourself to anyone dilutes the essence of who you are. Once you realize how truly unique and wonderful you are, the pressure to be/act/think like anyone else evaporates.

The true-you has conviction, determination, and confidence without arrogance or conceit. The authentic true-you is a resourceful, creative, loving, helpful, energetic, fun person. Learning from the past, looking to the future, living fully here and now.

You are in charge of defining your future self, so be kind. It's normal to compare strengths, weaknesses, possessions, looks, and more to others. It's part of the pattern recognition and learning process. This works great when we feel confident and see the big picture. But comparing your life to the highlights seen across the media sharpens the disconnect between fantasy and reality.

The path to remembering the true authentic you is different. It starts with trusting in your connection to a higher power, then clearly remembering what has worked or not worked, without judgment or comparison.

Getting out of your own way starts by stepping aside and observing what is happening between the ears. The true-you is the observer able to step back, recognize, and acknowledge the world does not change, we change.

~~~

When valuable time is spent chasing shortcuts we never quite reach the self-acceptance we seek. Observing instead of comparing gets you beyond the desire to want what other people have or to judge their lifestyle. Being happy with what you have, perfectly, in the moment, is the most prized feeling of all.

Building a great life reflection starts with slowing down long enough to look in the mirror honestly. It really doesn't matter who you are or what your station in life is, when you relax into yourself the world is perfect. Being yourself, warts and all, strikes an authentic chord with people. It relaxes the need to compare or conform. It places the perception of self-worth squarely on the shoulders of the owner.

The root of the word "*authentic*" is author; to be the intentional author of your life is to live authentically. Maybe you made some bad choices, missed some opportunities, or were trapped in circumstances that left some scars. Scars, both physical and emotional, detail where we were, but not who we can be. As the author of your life don't expect to get it right by accident or even on the first draft. It is a work-in-progress. Rather than mastering life try mastering your mind.

I've found that remembering the true-you is a lot like playing a guitar. When first fingering a new chord it feels awkward. Trying to find the strum rhythm seems impossible; it is tempting to give up. Come back to it the next day and that chord falls into place a little easier, the strum delivers glimpses of a good rhythm. Stay with it for a week or so and an amazing thing happens. All of a sudden you're playing a new tune! Even though it may not sound like the original, or quite like you want, it's yours and feels good. Relaxing into yourself is the same process.

Understanding your natural strengths, abilities, and weaknesses is vital to knowing which policies to put into place. Consider for a minute how different everybody is. No two people are alike. No two people will make the same decisions, even under the exact same circumstances. Nobody enjoys the unique combination of personality, music, taste, etc., as you.

It has taken a long time to honestly observe and accept my unique self. It is an ongoing process of accepting circumstances, being thankful for everything, then learning to treat the body/mind as a canvas for artful living.

One time while traveling, I stumbled on a copy of the book, "*Jonathan Livingston Seagull,*" by Richard Bach and had the time to read it under a shade tree. It's a funny little book about a seagull that gets thrown out of the flock for flying differently. He tried to fit in and live by the flock's routines but just couldn't.

His struggles lead him down the path of gull-discovery to an elegant definition of wisdom. Jonathan realized that the only way to live was to pursue his love of flying while helping others do the same. The great gull showed him that heaven lives here on earth in the process of perfecting the true-you. The book made it clear that how you live is more important than what you live for.

~~~

The challenge is that you can't use the mind to change the mind, as much as you may want to, it's impossible. Escape the bondage of thought by accepting all that you are. Stop planning and get busy living. To feel successful, you don't have to be perfect, copy anyone, or change who you are, just become more of your best self. By being the best version of yourself you become happier, the world becomes your playground and a better place for all.

Make the choice to focus on developing what YOU have to offer and release the need to gain external approval. When you release feelings of frustration, wanting, or fear there's more time to be you. The meaning we seek is about finding ways to express your unique self within the context of your surroundings.

While gently remembering the authentic true-you remember to go easy on yourself. It took 20, 30, 40, 50 years to get to where you are; getting back to your true self probably won't happen overnight. The path forward appears when you relax into what is, then harness the power of emotional fire to move forward filling needs with intention.

Wisewords: *"Be yourself, everyone else is taken"* ~Oscar Wilde

≈ Embrace your Inner Fan

Do you believe your mind has the power to change your body? Your relationships? Your reality? Even though this concept has been proven many times, we still can doubt our own power. Thoughts create things. Thoughts are things. Realizing the true-you starts with silencing the stinkin' thinkin' of fear, desire, and negativity by embracing your "*inner-fan.*"

We all have at least two identities inside our head talking all the time, the inner-critic and the inner-fan. These ego voices battle through the thought talk monologue about beliefs, skills, lovability, and every aspect of self worth. The inner-critic is driven by what psychologists call ANTs, automatic negative thoughts.

This ANT programming accumulates over the years of being told what's normal, how to dress, where to go, what to fear and strive for, whom to love, and how to live. Trying to conform to these norms creates ANT chatter that conflicts with our real nature. ANT thoughts are based on feelings of fantasy, fear, and scarcity.

The inner-critic ego has been seduced by desire. It takes things personally by feeling attacked, suppressed, taken for granted or ignored. It spins doubt into a web of reactions instead of responses. It even worries about and regrets things that didn't happen. The word automatic can be replaced with unaware. Without awareness the ANTs tell stories and make up stuff that entertain fears. This promotes self-defeating beliefs and behaviors. Here is some typical inner-critic ANT chatter:

"No." / "This will never work out" | "I wish I had _____ in my life"

"I should have invested in _____" | "Everyone else is having all the fun"

"I don't think I can do this" | "I deserve better"

"As soon as I accomplish _____ I'll be able to relax/be happy..."

"I need love/approval/ _____ to feel good about myself"

"_____ doesn't like/care about me/is out to get me"

"I know something bad will happen" | "It's my fault." / "It's not my fault"

"I don't care"

The other voice is your inner-fan, guardian angel, cheerleader, and constant supporter calling. It understands that other people and even our own mind will act badly at times, but doesn't compare or take it personally. These kind-mind life-affirming thoughts are in harmony with the true-you: they reflect on accomplishments and hold your win-list in mind.

The win-list is everything that has worked out well in the past, feels right now, and helps visualize an inspired future of healthful living, social connection, and creative expression. It starts by accepting what is actually happening then builds out gratefully toward what's next. Inner-fan win-list thoughts are the opposite of worry and stress.

Stress is the inner-fans way of telling you that something is wrong. When you find yourself stressed it's usually because you're trying too hard to do something that doesn't truly serve your soul. Your fan will let you know when you're compensating with addictions or unhealthy behaviors, but you have to listen.

Your fan holds the keys to your future. It is a friend with your best interests at heart. It picks the people and places that make you smile. It releases guilt and encourages selfless interdependence. Pick up and listen carefully to the guidance it speaks, for it is the voice of your truth. It knows your highest purposes and has the answers to all your questions. It says things like:

"Yes." / "Sure let's go for it."

"I'm grateful and happy with my life as it is."

"I'll learn from my mistakes but won't dwell on them."

"I got this."

"I know _____ didn't mean to hurt me."

"I'm not sure how to do it but I'm willing to try."

" I feel good about myself because I know I did my honest best."

Both voices are real and in competition for your attention. There is a Cherokee legend of a grandfather talking to his grandson: "*My son, there is a battle between two wolves inside us all. One is evil. It is anger, jealousy, greed, and resentment. The other is good. It is joy, love, hope, humility, kindness, empathy, and bravery.*" The boy thought about it, and asked, "*Grandfather, which wolf wins?*" The old man quietly replied, "*The one you feed.*"

Telling yourself tired, sad or stupid stories is feeding the bad wolf. When you catch yourself thinking a story based on fears or negative expectations throw down a hard stop. Reboot and shift back to the win-list. Worry is a waste of good imagination power. Most of the things we worry about are not true or never happen.

It takes skill and energy to balance the tension of these opposite voices. An unaware ego throws past successes out and focuses on what's missing, the mistake list. Building up an ongoing win-list dialog starves negative thoughts of attention until they fade into background balance. Brilliant things happen inside calm minds. The simple process of slowing the thought train creates an opportunity to jump off and feed the good wolf.

~~~

Thoughts of sex, love, sports, news, addictions, dreams, gratitude, to-do's and more are constantly rattling around our minds. Just below the surface are the important recurring tones, the ones questioning reality and self-worthiness. Each and every one an opportunity to draw you closer or pull you further away from personal harmony.

The voices in your head are always playing ping-pong. The average person has 60,000 thoughts per day, that's almost 50 thoughts per minute! About 95% of them are repeating over and over.

Some of these dialogs deal with managing and planning daily activities: what to wear, where to eat, what's on TV, who to text, what to post. They repeat lyrics from songs and make judgments on others.

But the human mind can only hold one thought at any time. It's true, it may seem like a swirling maze of voices but is really just one after another switching dialogs real fast. There is a limited amount of time for thoughts to happen each day. Trying to avoid painful thoughts actually brings them on. You can't believe everything you think.

As you consciously trigger good thoughts it cuts back on the time/space available for bad thoughts to exist. Learning to quiet the mind and being aware that thoughts happen one at a time, one after another delivers the ability to slow the chatter then catch, feel, reinforce, and feed supportive thoughts, your win-list.

A thought is the only thing with real power to make things happen in the world. Every single thought has either a positive or negative charge that attracts or repels personal harmony. Every thought spoken by your fan, is one not spoken by the critic. Policy is about helping your mind choose which ones to speak, listen to and build on.

One way to notice the negative voices is that they often speak in black and white, make things up, avoid the present, regret the past, place expectations on the future, focus on challenges, play victim, take things personally, feel guilty, or blame others.

This is inner-critic ego ANTs corrupting files, spinning lies, making up stories, and steering decisions in the wrong direction. Simply noticing them weakens their power. Stop jumping to judgment of yourself and others. Every thought is an opportunity to seek truth, have a chat with the fan, to send a blessing and move on.

~~~

Everything begins with a thought. Art, a relationship, habits, a song, a skyscraper, all are thoughts grown into reality. The Dhammapada (one of the core texts of Buddhism), tells us the same thing: "*Our life is shaped by our mind; we become what we think.*"

The story of Buddha demonstrates this idea nicely. Buddha was a man who knew there was more to life than wealth and pleasure. He was obsessed with finding the path to a peaceful mind and decided to abandon privilege to seek inner peace. His long battle with Mara, the Lord of Desire, sheds light on the how to find and fund the inner-fan.

After years of trying rituals and following gurus, Buddha let go of the search, looked inward and found peace in the acceptance of both suffering and success, the middle way. He learned that to keep it real you have to deal. Buddha adopted policies of yoga and meditation to tame and train his mind to see differently. The rest, as they say, is history. All lives are stories of hope, challenge, courage, redemption, and grace. Every story matters.

~~~

The inner-critic often comes at you with a loud, anxious wanting saying *"I should…" "I need to…" and "I wish…"* This is the voice of desire and control. To build up the inner fan dismiss the inner-critic. Say goodbye to the voice that judges.

Say adiós to the tongue saying it cannot be done, you are not good enough, it's too hard, it won't work.

One way to get around the critic is to use conscious self-talk. Try referring to yourself by name or "*you*", instead of "*I.*" When we use external pronouns it takes some self-judgment pressure off and pulls the critic to the side. By viewing yourself as a separate person it's easier to give ourselves more objective advice. As an example to calm anxiety instead of "Why am I nervous?" try using "Why are you nervous?" When faced with challenges the answer is always, "__(your name)__, you can do this."

Or try the imaginary friend technique. Picture someone like yourself giving you positive, uplifting advice then take that advice as if it came from a trusted source. With practice and awareness it becomes easier for the inner observer to spot, then gradually dismiss ANTs from awareness.

This process of self-awareness is called a practice and not a perfect because there is no perfect. There will always be a duality of voices begging for attention. Feeding the inner-fan helps pick which ones to listen to and which ones to ignore.

While writing this book, many months passed with no feedback on progress. My inner-critic would say things like "*I can't do this,*" and "*it's no good, forget it, move on.*" I learned to rig the game by setting timely deadlines for editorial review. This way when the voice appeared I was able to say, "*real feedback is coming, go away.*"

An amazing thing happens when you drop negative (painful) thinking and decide to stay positive. The world begins to support and encourage you. Just as plants can't grow in darkness, people can't shine without light. The thinker and the thought are married for life; building a good relationship between the two is essential. As you learn to cooperate with your own mind negativity evaporates. Positive thoughts are the batteries that power your love light so others can see and support you.

Wisewords: *"Carefully watch your thoughts before they become your words, manage and watch your words for they become your actions, consider and judge your actions as they will become your habits, acknowledge and watch your habits for they become your values, understand and embrace your values for they will become your destiny."* ~Mahatma Gandhi

≈ Understanding Needs

Managing modern living is a moving target. Figuring out where to spend your precious time and resources can be hard. You may, like me, have spent years chasing random wants then feeling confused and unable to zero in on needs. Our challenge is figuring out true needs and mapping a path to satisfy them.

Solving the mental tug-of-war between striving and savoring is not as obvious as it seems. We are trained to strive for accomplishment and success by gathering data, making goals, working, holding on, seeking, and pushing for what we think we should do, want or deserve. Savoring is the balancing force. It is the ability to slow down, let go, enjoy life as it is and allow things to unfold. We all need both. Happiness matters. Working toward goals is as important as enjoying the fruits of your labors.

Just about everything holds some element of both. For example yoga takes physical effort, but offers rewards of a calm mind. A good job is still work, but delivers socialization and financial rewards. With awareness, effort and enjoyment, wanting and relishing, become the same thing.

Contentment, happiness, and peace of mind have very little to do with circumstances of birth or how hard one tries. It has everything to do with addressing true needs. More success in one area (money) does not make up for a lacking in another (health, relationships, creativity, fun…). When you slow down and pay attention, true needs become obvious.

This awareness delivers the knowingness that success can come with arrogance or humility. Mindless success blows ego entitlement up like a peacock strutting around "*look at me look at me,*" but never really feeling great about it. Mindful success crosses over with a humble whisper of "*thank you*" as you happily get back to doing whatever it is you need to do.

This approach acknowledges that most minds operate about the same way. The contents may be different but our essence is the same, not so deep down we all have similar needs. When you make the time to understand your own mind you will better understand the minds and needs of others as well.

No discussion of balancing needs would be complete without the insight of positive psychology pioneer Abraham Maslow. Dr. Maslow believed, as do I, that we all have the capacity to be fully alive on our own terms, our own personal park, something he called self-actualization. To move up his ladder demands that needs at each level are met before moving on, no skipping steps.

At the bottom of the hierarchy are the basic human needs: food, water, air, sleep, and sex (yes, Maslow said sex is a basic need). The next level is all about security and stability: physical security, family security, home security, employment, and health.

Once individuals have basic connection, nutrition, shelter and safety, they can relax and attempt to accomplish more. The third level is the psychological needs of tribe, friendship, community, intimacy, and connection, to share one's self with others. The fourth level of needs, esteem, is achieved when individuals feel good, competent, and recognized for what they have accomplished.

At the top of the pyramid is the need for self-actualization. This occurs when we reach a state of harmony, peace, and acceptance of the realities of life. This is a place of understanding and creativity as you live near your full authentic potential and help others do the same. Maslow believed that to feel complete, to live in your park, these needs are non-negotiable.

Lens of Perception & Mindfulness Orientation

Maslow was right on the mark but forgot to factor in one important human tendency: social conformity. A lot of people don't want to stand out, be judged as different or perceived as lucky. We try to fit in to gain approval or acceptance. Everyone likes to be liked. Sometimes we try too hard to gather that affection.

The problem with fitting in is that we don't trust our individual mix of situation, talents, and personal style. In an effort to fit in we forget ourselves. We spend energy denying desires and supporting other people's version of reality. There are plenty of depressed rich people and tormented celebrities to prove this point.

When you put together psychology and personal-growth, the path to peace-of-mind lies in defining your own reality and measure of success. If wealth or status does it, then go for it. Maybe artistic accomplishment, volunteering, or deeper relationships would serve you better. Only you can tell.

Needs change over time. What once worked may no longer serve you. The striving/savoring mix changes throughout the different stages of life.

All the motivational books in the world will not deliver lasting personal growth without acceptance of reality, personal honesty, surrender, the fire of desire, and a plan to express yourself. It's not enough think about goals and potential. To make it reality you need to live it.

It's like physical exercise, if you do it, it works. If you quit, it stops working. There is no point in the pursuit of self-discovery where you can stop and say, I have it. It's an ongoing process of discovering the needs of self and others, showing up then managing highs & lows.

If you stay grateful for what is, mine new ideas, try refining approaches, build skills, and stay mindful of true needs, you will create a continuously better and more satisfying version of your authentic self.

Wisewords: *"Life is not a popularity contest. Be brave, take the hill, but first answer the question: "What is my hill?"* ~Matthew McConaughey

≈ The Reality Zone

I used to believe that reality existed in the world around me. Experts, schools, teachers, reporters, corporations, and spiritual counselors, all would say what is "*real*" and consequently, how to deal with that reality.

Following opinions, advice, beliefs, and instructions cater to our natural tendency to do what is expected, respect authority and to take others at their word. But these second-hand perceptions of reality are misleading.

It seems that reality is much more of a subjective thing based on perception and expectations, It's quite different for everybody. When you feel the reality of your life is better than expected you feel happy. When reality appears to be worse than the expected, welcome to unhappy.

The only reality that matters is the one in your mind's eye. Only when things are right in your head can you feel content and be of service to others. In a very real way, you are the center of your galaxy, but also part of a much larger universe.

Welcome to your world brought to you by the voices inside your head. We all have a running dialog with inner thoughts that psychologist Sigmund Freud believed drives the subconscious mind. This banter generally creates encouraging fan (I can…) or discouraging critic (I can't…) thoughts. Too often it gets stuck in *"I'm special and deserve..."* thinking.

Stop. Wake up. You are special, but not entitled to anything beyond what you create. Unrealistic expectations lead to arrogance. Media overload fuels expectations that pull our mind out of the reality zone. I can't tell you how much energy I've wasted trying unsuccessfully to get reality to conform to my vivid media-fueled imagination. I've found that when you become aware of thoughts and challenge irrational beliefs you begin to have some control over where they take you.

What is important? Better health? Closer friendships? More financial resources? What do you want? What do you need? What life upgrades will deliver more satisfaction now and over the long-term? You may be a legend in your own mind, but the world rewards and remembers those who give, not those who take. Find ways to get what you need by giving to others and everything will fall into place.

Figuring out the meaning of life is more about learning how to get your mind to perceive reality in a clear and comfortable way. Like any good game, this one has pieces and rules. The pieces of the reality zone are acceptance, mindfulness, and gratitude.

Acceptance: Seeing behaviors and situations as they truly are gets you squared in the reality zone. Acceptance of reality serves to evaporate any rationalization, blame, or victim thinking. Once you realize that you give everything you see all its meaning, and that meaning drives feelings, the situation becomes clear: it's all in your mind. You are the cause and the cure. If you want to feel good you must create expectations that accept reality.

Mindfulness: There are lots of variations on the definition of this concept. Consciousness, empathy, observing feelings from a distance, not judging thoughts, living in the moment, awakening to experience, paying attention, monotasking. Mindfulness means something slightly different to everyone. It is less about changing the mind and more about changing our perspective of mind, learning to be at ease the way it is.

Think about mindfulness as the beliefs bridge between the conscious and subconscious. It is both a skill and a measure of the ability to calm the monkey mind, focus thoughts, manage expectations, and take a nonjudgmental stance while balancing the needs to strive and savor.

Everybody has some conflicting thoughts (lust vs. love, greed vs. giving, good vs. bad, yes vs. no, and so on). Both camps want you. Mindfulness gives you some influence over which camp gets more attention.

Mindfulness reminds that how you do anything is how you do everything. It is the confluence of self-control, expectations, beliefs, and awareness. It reconciles all the forces pushing in on you, and all the energy inside wanting to push out. When you honestly pay attention, mindfulness helps spot inconsistencies between the thoughts that are working and those that are not.

The more mindfulness you are able to muster, the better you can filter out the noise. Practicing occasional mindfulness leads to a more consistent awareness. Consistent awareness creates lasting change.

One technique for raising mindfulness of thoughts is the ABC process (Activate, Beliefs, Consequences). As a thought or desire presents itself, triggering some emotion, zoom out and run through the ABC's:

• Activate awareness: Stop and ask what caused it? How do you feel?

• Beliefs: Review what attachment baggage the thought carries. Is it rational or irrational?

• Consequences: Feel what the thought implies (positive or negative) then make smart choices.

What you think is what you believe. Beliefs lead to expectations. Expectations define results. Your custom mindfulness software scans for what's important, filters the options, and factors consequences until thoughts can be focused, choices made, and actions taken. It has been shown to drive overall well-being by helping to stay less anxious, depressed, or impulsive. It brings higher self-awareness, esteem, vitality, and general happiness.

Some of the decisions we make today will have a tremendous impact on what we find in our lives tomorrow. Mindfulness is the accumulation of all you are and all you hope to be, centered in the present moment. It guides priorities, thoughts, words, and actions creating tomorrow today. It turns hope into happening.

Gratitude: This is the most important skill and way of being that can be cultivated over a lifetime of living and learning. Gratitude stitches the themes and threads of an evolving life together. It delivers clues to the inner-workings of the true-you.

The rules of the reality zone are:

1. You are the boss (of your mind).
Forget about comparing your life to anyone else's. You must devise your own future. No one else can, but they will try. Learn from others but don't worry about what they think.

2. Doing your best is enough.
Doing your best means doing what you can, when and where you can, to express yourself and make a difference. It implies an understanding of what's possible then guides you in setting realistic goals at a manageable pace. You may still have to push

yourself to do the things you know you need to do, but it will be against a sensible standard. Don't confuse this with doing enough to get by. Doing your best demands an honest self-awareness against a personal standard. Doing your best is enough to feel good about yourself.

3. Want what you have.

Get out of your head and into your heart. Savor everything gratefully (especially the little things). No matter what is going on, give thanks. Let honesty guide expectations of yourself and others. Reach up to people who might know more. Reach down to those that you can help. Build your tribe by helping outsiders become insiders. Stick by them. Find ways to worry less, live more, love freely and give of yourself. There is conditional love (of self) and unconditional love (of everything), one limits the mind, the other sets it free.

~~~

A look at the policy pillars through the lens of the reality zone reveals the decisions we made in the past have a fading impact on the present situation. The choices we make now will have a growing impact over time. Indecision and regret echo in both directions. The sweet spot is right now.

There are a thousand excuses or rationalizations for slipping out of the reality zone. All are major roadblocks to your own sense of happiness and well-being. Our creative minds will run wild without the guidance of a reality leash. Awareness delivers the presence to let go when things are over, and know when to prepare for what's coming next. People seem to slip out of reality when they are afraid of being taken advantage of or feel they are not getting the respect they deserve.

Dwelling on what others seem to have, past pain and blaming anyone, even when we know it wasn't their fault, keeps our mind in turmoil. We tell ourselves, "*I worked so hard I deserve _____ (more money, better job, friends, love, recognition...)*" even when it doesn't really matter. It only seems like everyone else is getting ahead and having all the fun; they're not. Releasing desire is personal and the only battle worth fighting.

We go on power trips or take things personally, then forget to pivot when we realize we were wrong. We let unrealistic expectations of ourselves and others be the gauge of success. We allow past hurts to set limits on how much joy we allow ourselves to experience now. The reality zone blurs when we use one standard to judge ourselves and another to place judgments on others.

It seems like just about everybody repeats some version of this victim story to himself or herself: I don't have enough of X, Y, or Z. Nobody knows what I'm going through. I feel helpless. I'm not getting the attention /support/resources/love I need. Sometimes we tell these stories long enough that we actually believe them.

It is amazing how we create stories and accept them as truth often when there is no basis in reality. We invent things to fear or worship so we don't have to look at the real mystery inside our mind. Looking inward reveals not what we think, but who we are. Part of our glorious human nature is to expand as a person and overcome limits. It's the life you live, the people you touch, and the work you do from the inside out that matters.

~~~

To be happy let go of the desire to judge, win, or dominate. Let go of the self-assigned responsibility to change or fix anyone. When you are irritated or annoyed, look inward. Ask yourself what the real problem is? When in doubt, don't go to some tired old story or rationalization for comfort. Getting mad at any annoyance is really just a drain on personal energy. Release control then ask, *"what can I be doing differently?"*

The simple act of asking for guidance releases the suffocating grip of entitlement or a need to control, it brings clarity to any situation. Clarity dictates perspective and perspective dictates our experience. For a better life experience always work towards more clarity.

The reality zone, much like gratitude, is a frame of mind supporting the lens of perception. Rationalizations and petty ego goo are scrubbed away, leaving a clear lens on real life. Everything is honestly acknowledged, experienced, and dealt with. The good stuff, the bad stuff, everything.

Shift from victim to victor by seeing situations clearly, then looking for ways to contribute. Communicate your needs and feelings. Listen carefully, ask for clarity, and look for solutions that allow everyone to win. If, in the end, middle ground cannot be reached, be prepared to follow your own path of integrity, for this is the only path to a peaceful mind.

~~~

You may be surprised to know that you have total control over the four things shape your reality zone: attitude, motivation, habits, and time. All of these are ruled by the subconscious. This is where ninety-five percent of thoughts loop in the background. These thoughts behind the thoughts are the real captain of your ship, reinforcing beliefs, and steering decisions.

The subconscious is connected through intuition to a larger well of wisdom, which offers answers to all of life's questions. Policies work consciously in the subconscious to ask the right questions, rewire outdated beliefs, and keep thoughts positive so that good decisions can happen naturally. Setting your mind up to work for you is what I call rigging the game. This idea is more about the game than the rigging. Sure you want to win, but learning to play is enough.

The game of life has lots of pieces. Stuff we think and do moves them around the board. To play the game you need skills, shields, a quest and lots of energy. You can't play alone, you will have allies and enemies. The challenges are endless and emotional resistance is real. Once on top you will be knocked down and have to start climbing again. That's it. Rigging the game means to accept these rules and decide to play anyway.

If you ponder these elements of transformation, undertake a sincere self-evaluation, and keep beliefs fluid, you will find that in everything, you always have a choice. The key to rigging the game is knowing which battles to pick, when to pivot, and not ever giving up on fulfilling true needs.

~~~

Sometimes the game requires you to put yourself in situations opposite of what you really want (or need) to do. For example, during the times when I felt unable to write, I would take jobs as a handyman. Long days of heavy work would tend to soften my resistance and push me back into the writer's chair.

Challenges are put in our way not to stop us, but to call out our courage and strength. We often resist getting on the path to genuine well-being because it seems long, hard, and uncertain. In my experience, it's the only way. The skill lies in learning to enjoy the ride.

Personally I have often resisted doing the things and making the changes that deep down I know needed to be made. In Star Trek, the Borg say *"resistance is futile"* and they mean it. Maybe another ten thousand years of evolution will lead humans to the same conclusion, but who has time for that? All rivers lead to the sea, and all personal growth techniques lead to policies. The only real problems boil down to figuring out paths to satisfy genuine needs. Once you feel and believe in the process you will know more about who you are and what you are capable of.

The only thing stopping you from being present is wanting to be somewhere else. It's that wanting feeling that derails wellness. What we do have is right now, a place where you don't expect more than reality can deliver, and you don't settle for less than you deserve. It is a place free from rationalization, where the rich, juicy, really good living happens.

Wisewords: *"The shortest and surest way to live with honor in the world is to be in reality what we would appear to be"* ~Socrates

≈ The Personal Policy Institute (PPI)

To help shape happening habits, log onto the *"Putting Wisdom to Work"* companion website. The Personal Policy Institute is a place to find ideas, tools, and techniques. It is an open-source virtual think tank dedicated to creating, compiling, and sharing the best approaches to thriving.

Free downloads of the activities covered in this book: PolicyPillars.com.

Companion Guide Life Skill Solutions

Personal Policy Report Card (PPRC) PDF: Zero in on strengths + areas for growth

Gratitude Garden PDF: Plant and feed the seeds of a kind mind

Ulysses Contract PDF: Mindfulness map sets intentions into action

Journey Journal PDF: Track, connect, share, and celebrate

Group Intention Circle: Facilitator guide

Breathing Meditation Technique

Rig the game with BeSMART Goals

Create policy from the Tao Te Ching

Affirmations, Quotes, Maxims, and more

Join the email forum to receive mindful moments and policies as they are released.

Personalized assistance on completing activities available.

To share is to care. Please add your experience and tips on putting wisdom to work by adding the #pw2w hash tag to online posts and reviews.

2. Five Pillars

It takes a good map to navigate the highway of life, to know which roads to take then spot exits and destinations when they do appear. Building a guidance system delivers confidence in making good decisions. The policy pillars are a way to get priorities organized so important needs do not get missed.

Some lifestyle areas may be working well, masking the fact that others are lacking. It's easy to get stuck relying on what we are good at, even when we know we are capable of much more. Whatever path you are on, there is room for improvement and time to adjust course.

Balancing the mix of needs, wants, actions, and opportunities is the journey we are all on. One challenge in getting priorities straight is too often success is gauged against external measures such as appearance, approval, achievement, and affluence.

There are lots of problems with valuing yourself by comparing to others. Appearance will always go downhill. Approval makes you a slave to the opinions of others. Achievement will keep you chasing the never-ending to-do list. Affluence tricks you into thinking net worth equals self worth. Success has to come from within.

To help get and keep priorities straight the policies are organized under five pillars. This grouping is intended to expand, hold, and order the needs that fill most lifestyle situations. The five policy pillars are:

· Healthful living: Getting the mind and body in alignment with reality.

· Satisfying Relationships: Feeling engaged/connected to others and a higher power.

· Abundant Resources: Building and managing resources.

· Accepting Responsibility: Taking care of yourself and others. To feel needed.

· Playful Creativity: Releasing creativity and being sure to have enough fun.

How are you doing? If you answered one hundred percent yes to all of these then you get it. Give this book away and get on with it. If there is any hesitation or curiosity about what might be possible, read on.

Rounding out your pillars is a process for self-discovery and will be a trip through uncharted territory. The idea is that when needs become priorities and responsibilities are met, you can feel complete and good about yourself, no matter what the outcome. When the pillars are all addressed you create the conditions to thrive.

The personal policy approach drops judgment or expectation and gathers each unique human experience under the pillars. It is a framework to prioritize needs and maintain mindfulness on the big picture. The pillars metric tells us when to work, relax, or celebrate.

Learning to express true human nature while living in harmony in the world demands keeping it real. In the reality zone hopes, skills, and ambitions match up with needs, options, resources, and community.

To be realistic is to be honest with yourself and others while doing your best at everything you do decide to do. Keeping it real is not always easy. You must be willing to embrace uncertainty to try new ways of being before knowing what will happen. You must be willing to be a solution.

Realistic people can dream big, but those dreams are rooted in the reality of an honest life story. Personal policies supporting balanced pillars help you get beyond idealism and imitation, to see reality, accept the limitations, reach just beyond the comfort zone and get on with creating your good life.

I wrote this book because I wanted to know more about how life works. I needed to make sense of the thoughts, feelings, and situations that surrounded me. I wanted to change some outdated behaviors and get real with myself. I wanted to stop searching, relax and get busy living my best possible life.

I discovered that when I tune out the noise and open my eyes to see how life actually does work, priorities become clear. Trusting in this process as a natural reflex leads to a stronger yet more supple personal power.

Adopting a policy-based lifestyle demands a thirst for knowledge and a love of learning. It gets easy with practice. Policies challenge you to change the things you can and stop worrying about the things you can't. As you remember and reclaim yourself, tired habits fall away, creating a personal park.

Wisewords: *"Wisdom is knowing what to do next, skill is knowing how to do it, and virtue is doing it."* ~ David Starr Jordan

> Activity: Policy Pillar Report Card (PPRC)

We all need a little help tuning out static, focusing on priorities and making life transitions. The PPRC is designed to raise awareness of what might need fixing and how to approach change. At the end of each pillar section below you will have an opportunity to take a priorities inventory. This activity helps identify blind spots and paint a path forward even when there is no clear solution or goal.

It is easy to rely on strengths to compensate for weaknesses. Think of the PPRC as a reality zone grade, a needs review, a way to see rough spots and get guidance on priorities. Your numbers will give you instant feedback on what is strong and what could use some improvement.

This is not a "*happiness*" scale and there is no "*good*" or "*bad*" score. It is a measure of self-awareness and a tool to help focus energy on satisfying evolving core needs. Apply some policies then revisit quarterly to track progress.

≈ The Health Pillar

The philosopher Aristotle once said, "*You can never have too much health, friendship, love, wisdom, or self-esteem.*" I don't think it was an accident that he placed health first in this list. There are so many aspects to a healthful living: physical health, spiritual health, and mental health. All critical to you being the best you. Without health, what do you have?

The five pillars are interconnected; good mental and physical health is often a result of responsible decisions, good relationships, and creative use of resources. By making the health pillar strong you've made a smart foundation decision that supports all personal policies. A strong health pillar can help you live longer, have more energy, be more connected, reduce stress, and have a lot more fun. The health pillar includes:

· Physical health: Diet, exercise, weight, sleep, etc.

· Mental health: Acceptance, resiliency, attitude, impulse control, etc.

· Social health: Regular meaningful interactions with others, etc.

· Spiritual health: A connection to your higher power, meditation, etc.

Of the list above it seems most people spend the majority of time investing in physical health by going to the gym, trainer, classes, diets, etc. Giving mental, social and spiritual health some attention delivers real rewards as well.

As with everything, health is relative to one's unique life, body, experiences, and attitude. There is no point in comparing your situation to anyone else's; focus on what you need to do to feel the best you can, then do it. Eat nutritious food, avoid sedentary work, exercise the body and mind, nurture a spiritual connection, practice self-control, feed relationships, live responsibly. Everyone will serve these needs in different ways, but serve them we must.

There have been enough studies done to prove beyond a shadow of a doubt taking care of yourself pays off big-time. Exercise, yoga, meditation all increase energy, improve memory, calm anxiety/depression, reduce risk of cancers, curb cravings for crappy food, and so much more.

People with a healthy mindful disposition have less body fat and better heart health. By holding awareness of thoughts and feelings, naturally good choices happen more often. Learning to spot and adopt good policies that strengthen the pillars is a skill and a process, not a destination. As life changes, health policies must change as well. Stay fluid and tuned in to what is working for yourself and others.

Here are some Health policies that seem to work well:
- Eat and snack on low-fat food as a habit.
- Cut way back on carbs.
- Drink lots of water and juices.
- Skip the fries and soda.
- Exercise vigorously at least three times every week.
- Get plenty of sleep regularly.
- Skip the stress. Find healthy ways to relax.
- Expect good mental and physical health.

Health Maxim: Use it or lose it.

Health Affirmation – Repeated in the present tense with emotional feeling.

I take good care of myself. </> I enjoy good health.

(meditation key <:breathe in /:hold >:breathe out.

(Find more maxims, affirmations and meditation technique in Just Breathe and at PolicyPillars.com)

> **Health PPRC** – How well do you take care of your mind and body?

Instructions: Rate each item on a scale of one to ten, with one being low on awareness, satisfaction, or development and ten being high on that same scale. Be honest when rating yourself, and leave room for improvement. Scores of one are reserved for areas you don't think about much or are not aware of at all. Give yourself a two or three for factors you are aware of but need more information on or for some reason are not taking any action. Give yourself a four or five for occasional success/satisfaction. Scores of six, seven, or eight are for areas where you feel like you are "*getting it*," but know there you have more to do. Scores of nine and ten are reserved for areas you feel really good about and are ready to help others with. Once completed, you will have a score for each pillar and a scale to chart your growth progress.

_____ Attitude - Factors: optimist/pessimist, stress, hope, inner-fan/critic, other

_____ Diet/Weight - Factors: food choices, exercise, weight, body fat ratio, other

_____ Mind Fitness - Factors: meditation, hobbies, friends, games, laughter, other

_____ Sleep - Factors: Regular quality sleep.

_____ Addictions - Factors: Do you control them or do they rule you?

Score: _____ Grade: _____ Notes: _____

Health Pillar Grading: 5-20: D (weak, get moving) / 21-30: C (fragile, keep moving) / 31-40: B (good, but could be better) / 41-50: A (celebrate, strong, doing good, help others, aim for stronger)

Wisewords: *"Health is the greatest gift, contentment the greatest wealth, faithfulness the best relationship."* ~Buddha

≈ The Relationships Pillar

When asked to list the things in life that bring true joy, good relationships and social engagement always come out on top. We are all vibrating with the common cause of surviving, learning, loving, expressing and sharing ourselves while enjoying life. Whether it be neighbors, family, friends, co-workers, in person or online, it always comes back to community. Other people define our sense of place and purpose.

Fact of the matter is we are all in this together. Whether you like it or not, you are in relationship with everyone. Part of our purpose in life is about taking care of the people around you. The whole is greater than the sum of its parts. Having others to enjoy, learn from, to give to, to share success and challenges with, is key to feeling alive and fulfilled.

Stop and think for a second about how much joy family, friends, co-workers or a romantic partner bring to the daily routine. What are you doing to support your current people or make new connections? Relationships are experiments without promise of any outcome. Building connections means taking risks. They cannot be bought or sold, only given, received, and celebrated.

Even with all of the ways to connect and interact these days, or maybe because of them, there is an epidemic of loneliness across developing countries. This trend is a public health threat few people want to acknowledge or deal with. Most of us want deeper, richer relationships based on shared interests, goals, friends, and romance. We all want to feel special and needed. The question is how to go about it?

The best policy I've found to get good relationships on track is the golden rule: Do unto others as you would have done unto yourself. If you want people to listen and pay attention to you, you need to listen and pay attention to them. To be interesting, be interested. To be trusted, trust. This karmic law works great for people with strong self-esteem and self-love. But when we don't love ourselves 100% of the time we can treat ourselves, and others, badly.

Modern society is caught in an epidemic of self-absorption and lack of empathy. We want attention but don't know how to give it. Earning respect, support and best wishes comes from giving those to others. Making the time to listen and celebrate builds the social capital necessary to be heard and celebrated when your time comes. Research has actually proven that supporting others in their time of challenge and triumph totally elevates your mood and spirit.

This works both online and off. When someone bothers to post something online it means they're looking to share and would like some feedback. Social media is a fantastic place to chime in to celebrate others' successes, to contribute genuine praise, congratulations, or sympathy. For a deeper connection follow up on posts and conversations with curiosity, how is it going/working? Better yet go offline inviting friends into the real world for a meal or a walk to hear the full story.

There is a Swedish proverb that sums this attitude up: "*Shared joy is double joy; shared sorrow is half sorrow.*" This maxim reflects the wise belief that fostering connection and interdependence serves the individual and society as a whole. We all crave the comfort of connection. If you don't want resentment or to feel used quit keeping score. When you hold out, odds are you will miss out. Good relationship policies help us give and receive love freely.

~~~

It amazes me how often I have forgotten to let love be my guide. It's so easy to take people for granted or even sabotage relationships through meddling, envy, and jealousy. Even people I would consider to be my closest allies are sometimes victims of mindless, self-centered, or controlling behavior. Learning to let go of control, accept, give thanks for, and nurture others unconditionally feels great.

When you stop to think about it, we only know moments about other people, and they only know moments about us; the picture is always incomplete. We know very little about most of the people we spend the majority of our time with. We may know a little bit about coworkers', neighbors' and friends' current situation, but their past is mostly a mystery. We have tidbits of information about where they went to school, where they work and what some past relationships were like, but these are just snapshots compared to the full motion picture of someone else's life experience. There is always much more going on than meets the eye.

It's human nature to fill in the blanks and try to make situations conform to our wants. In doing this, we create a picture of the person that is really more a reflection of the person we think we want them to be, not who they are. The more we invest the time to communicate, enjoy, and share experiences with other people, the clearer they become. When you resist the urge to make up stories and allow others to be who they are instead of what you want them to be, you can have peaceful, honest relationships.

Genuine connection seems to take time. Even keen intuition can be derailed by assumptions or judgments. People are rarely who they appear to be on the outside. All you can really do is put your best foot forward, dig in with curiosity to find out what they are looking for and what problems they need help solving.

Acknowledge their awesomeness. Let go of expectation or control. Strive to leave people feeling better about themselves. Come from a place of openness and service, offer positive feedback, then see what gets reflected back. Stick with relationships that feel good and support your priorities. Let go of those that don't.

~~~

To help get relationship policies in place consider these ideas:

1. The village support system has broken down, creating a fractured society. People move and home becomes a phone number or email address. This often places too much dependency on the people we do see regularly. Without awareness, it's easy to place too many expectations or to try to control those we are closest to.

Usually there are two or three people across work, home, and recreation that we see regularly enough to depend on. Often we rely on our romantic partner to be our lover, best friend, financial partner, co-parent, trusted confidante, emotional companion, intellectual equal, our everything. That's a lot to ask.

Self-improvement is not all about you, it's also for the people around you. Stay conscious of how needy you can be. Look for ways to fill needs across several people and cut those close to you some slack if they don't always respond perfectly. True compatibility goes beyond shared likes. It is more about how you resolve the inevitable differences.

2. Don't take anything personally. A direct insult is rare, and rarely worth listening to. Most of the time, what we perceive as hurtful or an attack is just absent-mindedness or self-absorption. People are on their own trips and are rarely out to intentionally hurt each other. Some are just more aware of how their behavior affects others. Break free of the need for acceptance; opinions only count if you care. Learn

to accept and forgive without needing to reaffirm your own self-worth. Living well is the best revenge.

3. When someone close to you wins a prize, gets a promotion, finds romance, whatever, celebrate with them. Friends shouldn't respond to your good news with jealousy, indifference, or one-upmanship. It is so sad when we can't get out of our own way fast enough to be present with our people in their moments of joy. As the poet Oscar Wilde once said, *"Anyone can sympathize with the suffering of a friend, but it requires a very fine nature to sympathize with a friend's success."*

4. When in doubt, reach out. Think about all the times in life when you could have used a helping hand, some guidance or mentorship. Odds are there are people in your circle of influence who could benefit from your experience and expertise. An encouraging word or a helping hand can mean the world to someone. It's hard to ask for help so open the door and let people know you are there for them. Become a person of value by helping others.

5. Try to avoid becoming frustrated, upset, angry or irritated at others. Make a conscious decision to accept people as they are and expect others to accept you as you are. This will not always work out. Stressful emotions are often signals that something is out of balance and needs to change. Look within for answers. You may decide to change your orbit away from those who irritate you, but do it with love in your heart.

6. Treat your friends like family and vice versa. Don't take people for granted and don't forget the things others have done for you in the past. Interact without an agenda and consciously avoid wanting or trying to get away with anything. Stop trying to fit in and simply give your all. Expect nothing in return. Once free of expectation, relationships can flourish in the reality zone.

7. Conflict is inevitable. There is a time to fight for what you feel is right, and a time to surrender control. I've discovered it feels better to be happy than right. Every job and every relationship is going to demand communication and some compromise. When you feel inner conflict brewing, ask yourself: *"Am I fighting for my real needs here, or is this something I can let go of and get on with my life?"*

Beyond family, genuine lasting relationships are usually based on a shared bond or common interests. Work, romantic, creative, social - all relationships grow from the place where ideas, attitudes, and interests intersect. Look for areas where you can connect, show them your way, and consciously appreciate theirs. Consider approaching all relationships with the welcome mat out, supporting others' needs, and inviting them to play in your park.

Making connections starts with a name. People like to hear their name. Speaking names breeds familiarity. One personal policy that helps turn new acquaintances into friends is the name game. It works like this: while talking or soon after meeting someone that you want to remember their name, think of somebody else with the same name and a common trait. This mind triangulation is so simple and works every time.

I once met a fellow in the boatyard who seemed like someone I might like to sail with sometime. His name was Chris so I flashed on Christopher Columbus, both sailors. This is one way to rig the game, when I see him next and greet by name we can continue to build forward on our common interest.

The most important skill to building strong relationships is to get real with yourself. Getting real means stepping outside of ego long enough to clearly see how you appear to others, where you shine, and where you need some polish. This openness to the process of self-discovery helps build the wise confidence that secure people project.

Once you get comfortable with yourself, in your skin, with all gifts and challenges in clear view, the process of accepting and celebrating others can truly begin. Here are some relationship policies that seem to work well:
- Make an effort to attend family, educational, social, and spiritual activities even when you don't want to. You will usually end up feeling good that you went.
- Get out from behind the computer. Regularly schedule fun or interesting activities. Set up business meetings in-person away from the office.
- Make a birthday book with all the special dates including anniversaries and special occasions, then use that intelligence to tickle your special people with fond memories and well wishes.

Relationships Maxims:

Many hands make light work.

A smile for a stranger opens many gates.

A friend's eye is a good mirror.

Relationship Affirmations – Repeated in present tense with emotional feeling.

I AM love. </> I AM loved.

I trust. </> I am trusted.

I forgive. </> I am forgiven.

> Relationships PPRC – How well do you create & nurture your connections?

Satisfaction Scale: 1: Never 2: Low 3-4: Occasional 5-6: Semi-Regular 7-8: Regular 9-10: Complete

_____ Spiritual - Factors: clarity of belief, regular practice, shared experience, other

_____ Community - Factors: quality time, keeping in touch, exploring new, other

_____ Support - Factors: people who support/encourage you, clubs, activities, other

_____ Trusting (self/others) - Factors: See worst/best? Willingness to take risks, other

_____ Intimacy - Factors: friends, partner, work. Learn, celebrate, confide, other

Score: _____ Grade: _____ Notes: _____

Relationship Pillar Grading: 5-20: D (weak, get moving) / 21-30: C (fragile, keep moving) / 31-40: B (good, but could be better) / 41-50: A (celebrate, strong, doing good, help others, aim for stronger)

Wisewords: *"Who cares about the clouds when we are together? Just sing a song and bring the sunny weather."* ~Dale Evans

≈ The Resources Pillar

Does a rich man stranded on a tropical island need his money? Does a struggling young family need coconuts? Everybody's resource needs are different, and not always obvious. From an early age, we have been brainwashed to grab wealth, then consume and dispose. This model is good at filling up garages and landfills, but not so good at filling the soul. It's human nature to want more, but unconscious expectation inflation rigs the game against a peaceful, happy mind.

Resources boil down to people, time, money, knowledge, experiences, wisdom, and stuff. Which ones give you joy? Which do you have the power to develop or strengthen? What do you need to feel secure? Opening up to true resource needs delivers guidance on what to focus on. This can be a tricky idea to get your mind around in a consumer-based society.

It's no secret that life has become more complicated in developed or developing countries. The number of people on the planet has doubled over the last forty years, with no sign of slowing down. Population growth, energy depletion, financial needs, career, scattered families, gridlocked politics, and a changing global economy contribute to a reality where we demand more from fewer resources.

The ability to experience peace is not limited by circumstances but rather by a willingness to pause and listen. It seems the path to a peaceful mind is to know that more is not necessarily better. It's about focusing on quality, having enough, then spreading it around. Just like blood or water, resources need to keep moving.

Like it or not, money is the modern resource of choice. Learning how to manage it is an important skill that will bring some peace of mind and prepare you for some form of retirement one day. Beyond that, money in the bank is only as good as the experiences it can help you share with others. Research actually shows that when incomes grow over $70,000 per year people often experience decreasing pleasure and increasing stress. Money can't buy happiness, but adequate financial resources give you the time to explore other true needs, build lasting relationships and have some fun.

Let's take a closer look at what resources really are and how to manage them. Lasting resources include relationships, creative outlets, education, people, spirituality, experiences, and much more that will never be found in the mall. Beyond food and shelter, physical resources are merely stepping stones on the path of personal growth. Buried somewhere underneath everything you ever bought you will find the enduring things of real value. Taking inventory of your real resource needs opens doors to relieving the perceived pressure to accumulate stuff.

Research shows the "*high*" we get from buying things fades within twenty minutes of the purchase. It's easy to think buying things will bring lasting satisfaction, but it doesn't. Purchases often lead to a double dead end: debt, and a lot of junk cluttering up the closet.

The core components of the resources pillar include food, shelter, relationships, challenge, artistic outlets, values, education, family, friends, experiences, and money. There is no exhaustive list and everybody will need a different mix. Ask yourself which resources do you need to feel secure and which deliver true satisfaction, then you'll be on your way to defining long-term resource policies.

Here are some ideas that seem to work well:
- Appreciate what you have instead of focusing on what's missing.
- Stop buying stuff to compensate for weaknesses in other pillars.
- Learn about financial fitness and invest in the future.
- Invest (time and money) in personal growth and supporting others.

Resources Maxims:

Luck happens when preparedness meets opportunity.

A bird in the hand is worth two in the bush.

A penny saved is a penny earned.

Resource Affirmation – Repeated in present tense with emotional feeling.

I do my best </> I enjoy abundant resources.

> **Resources PPRC** – How effectively do you build and manage your resources?

Satisfaction Scale: 1: Never 2: Low 3-4: Occasional 5-6: Semi-Regular 7-8: Regular 9-10: Complete

_____ Home - Factors: safe, relaxing, affordable, convenient, other

_____ Financial - Factors: skills, sources of income, budget, investing, other

_____ Professional - Factors: job, lifestyle, career, challenge, rewards, other

_____ Material - Factors: needs met, wants realistic, other

_____ Wisdom - Factors: effort, research, mentors, expectations, other

Score: _____ Grade: _____ Notes: _____

Resource Pillar Grading: 5-20: D (weak, get moving) / 21-30: C (fragile, keep moving) / 31-40: B (good, but could be better) / 41-50: A (celebrate, strong, doing good, help others, aim for stronger)

Wisewords: *"Ask and it shall be given you; seek, and ye shall find; knock, and it shall be opened unto you."* ~Jesus

≈ The Responsibility Pillar

Taking full responsibility for your attitude, actions, and life situation is the key to empowerment. No more blaming work, parents, partners, etc. Stop telling stories to yourself and others. Responsibility mindfulness keeps you centered in the reality zone.

Being responsible feels good. It reminds us that when we focus on the happiness of others we are happier ourselves. It delivers that satisfied knowingness that you are living with integrity, having made good choices and done your best. Being responsible keeps it real. Responsibility is about doing the best you can, when and where you can.

Being responsible grants you the authority to take action when you see injustice, ignorance, or irresponsibility. As a member of any group, you must champion responsible decisions while guiding the organization to fair, sustainable policies, to do the right thing even when it is not popular.

Responsibility is the ethical backwind that reminds you the only thing lacking in any situation is what you're not giving. When you don't give your full effort, guidance, patience, understanding, flexibility, compassion, etc., you are somewhat responsible for any failure.

Taking responsibility when things go wrong instead of blaming something or someone else is empowering. The evolved human understands and accepts their role in all situations. Once you suit up, show up, stay open, tell others how to work with you, then actively participate, you have done your best and can feel good about whatever happens.

Responsibility awareness builds self-control. This pillar will help you quickly catch and quiet the thoughts that don't serve you. It cleans up the inconsistencies between the big true-you and the small ego-driven you. With practice, destructive, limiting, and whiney thoughts dissolve and disappear. The goal is a real-time gratitude awareness where wrong-thought exists less and less, then not at all.

Limiting smartphone use offers an opportunity to build responsibility awareness. This technology has changed our world and social dynamic. Gadgets offer tremendous convenience, power, and distraction. They are so easy to use that it's easy to obsess trying to possess all the goodies. They keep us in a safe bubble poking away at nothing often missing everything. Looking up to engage face-to-face is messy and takes effort. There is risk of embarrassment and rejection, but always worth it.

It's not about what you can get away with, because you can never get away from yourself. You get what you give. Cultivating a grateful mental garden then tending it with responsible thoughts always feels good and right. Accept responsibility not as a burden, but as a gift of belonging through interdependence.

Here are some responsibility policies that seem to work well:
- Slow down, stop, review the needs of all involved, then decide what to do.
- Always play it straight.
- Care for all living beings and the environment.
- Take yes and no seriously. Don't overpromise. Don't be flakey.

Responsibility Maxim: If you can't change your fate, change your attitude.

Responsibility Affirmation – Repeated in present tense with emotional feeling.
I AM the cause. </> I AM the cure.

> Responsibility PPRC – How well do you take care of yourself and others?
Satisfaction Scale: 1: Never 2: Low 3-4: Occasional 5-6: Semi-Regular 7-8: Regular 9-10: Complete

_____ Self - Factors: appreciate, trust, treat yourself well, self respect, other

_____ Purpose - Factors: invest in exploring, practice, other

_____ Service - Factors: help others, contributions, activism, mentoring, other

_____ Integrity/values - Factors: honest with self & others, behave ethically, other

_____ Others - Factors: awareness of wants/needs of all, ego, wisdom, other

Score: _____ Grade: _____ Notes: _____

Responsibility Pillar Grading: 5-20: D (weak, get moving) / 21-30: C (fragile, keep moving) / 31-40: B (good, but could be better) / 41-50: A (celebrate, strong, doing good, help others, aim for stronger)

Wisewords: _"Most people do not really want freedom, because freedom involves responsibility, and most people are frightened of responsibility."_ ~Sigmund Freud

≈ The Creativity Pillar

Psychologists have repeatedly shown that ninety-five percent of us test as creative geniuses between the ages of two to four years old. It's true; we're all born geniuses with the ability to connect concepts and create solutions at will.

Then something happens along the way. Other people's ideas of the way things work begin to influence our thinking. Parents, teachers, friends, family, TV, etc. impose fears and limits on our developing belief systems. By about age seven, only six percent of people continue to test as creatively gifted. The process of growing up fills our brain with limiting beliefs.

History celebrates the names of those who dared to let go of the tried and true. Picasso, Roosevelt, Curie, Einstein, Jobs. Each looked at the same things others were seeing but saw them in a different way. Creativity is about un-learning and giving yourself permission to let go of attachments to process and product. It unleashes the power of imagination to create extraordinary expectations.

By staying awake to creative solutions, you keep a door open to the wisdom of the universe. Creative thinking driven by policy priorities is a path to the true-you - an evolved, happy, healthy, interdependent person making the world a better place as you move through it.

People who stay creative have learned to think for themselves, reject limiting beliefs, and to trust hunches on how things can work. They believe in their ability to create successes large and small. Rather than fight the crowd trying to climb up the beaten path, creative people build bridges across or ladders down to where they want to go.

If necessity is the mother of invention, then playful creativity is the father. Developing and harnessing creative power is one key to unlocking the doors to personal success. Don't worry if you think you are not a creative person, you are. It might just take a little practice to recognize and remember your creative self.

Throughout history, many artists, writers, entrepreneurs, and people from all fields have recognized a source of creativity that is beyond explanation, impossible to describe, yet very real. This force has been called the universal superconscious, the well, being in the flow, the Unified Field. Creative people have learned to listen for clues, then work to turn those clues into clear ideas and action plans.

~~~

Creativity comes from following curiosity, developing skills, then letting the subconscious connect concepts. Creativity can be summoned by releasing ego control and simply asking for guidance then doing the work. Creativity releases the need for grand discoveries by letting small improvements add up.

Creativity is often thought of in regard to artistic or musical endeavors, but those represent only a small slice of the pie. Creativity is really just the process of connecting ideas to improve something or create something new. The more diverse your personal experience, knowledge and resources, the more creative connections you can make. Nature, art, music, family, work, recreation, anything can be a creative pathway to higher consciousness and a bridge to wisdom awareness.

Creativity can and should be applied to responsible decision-making, relationship building, lifestyle choices, resource building, etc. Often a simple creative solution will open doors that thousands of work hours could never unlock.

~~~

How many people do you know who talk about the projects they want to do or are working on but never seem to complete? Those who complete what they start stand out from the crowd because it is so rare. Getting good work done requires a plan, concentration, persistence, and creativity. Of these three, creativity is the most underdeveloped skill.

Staying conscious of your personal policies is a surefire way to tap creative resources on demand for amazing results. To start the creative juices flowing, break your ideas down to their basic steps (see BeSmart Goals below). Some of these will be as easy as making a call or putting something down on paper. Others may seem harder, with no apparent plan of attack. These are the ones to focus your creative energy on. Structure these as *"How can I..."* questions to get your subconscious working on specific answers.

The trick is to recognize insight when it appears. Even if it seems like a ridiculous solution or a vague, unformed idea, grab it and start building on the core concept. Keep a notepad, digital voice recorder or app on your phone. You never know what will spark a new idea. Often the missing piece of something you are working on falls into place when you least expect it, such as while exercising or driving.

Often shortly after a writing session, a missing piece pops into my head. Some people are blessed with perfect memories; I have a thought parade that pushes good ideas into the void along with the random mental chatter. A quick note captured on the recorder is like laying bricks one-by-one, building ideas from concepts into solid plans then a finished structure. It's how this book got written.

Creativity is just another muscle to flex and strengthen over time. Here are some ideas to help get the creative juices flowing:

1. Clear your workspace of clutter, only leaving the current project work on hand. Create mind space for creativity to happen by moderating obligations, meditating, recreation, etc. Let the question rattle around while taking a walk or cleaning the frig, anything non-analytical. Stop and lay bricks when inspiration surfaces.

2. Do some research, gather information, and set up a starting point. Nearly all creative work builds on something that already exists. As Pablo Picasso said, "*good artists borrow, great artists steal*." In either case, you, the life artist, needs to have a firm grasp of what has been done and what could be done to make it better. Watch documentaries and read insightful material. Talk with as many people as possible, paying attention for clues and insights you may not have considered. Make notes and let the ideas unfold. Ask for guidance when picking which ideas to pursue and listen for the subtle intuitive clues to keep on track.

3. Make focused chunks of time and eliminate disturbances by having already eaten (with leftovers ready), closing the door, turning off the phone (forget about Internet surfing or email). Reserve two to four hours of time to work on one thing to completion, or at least to get it to the next logical stopping point. One of the best times to do this is in the morning when you are fresh and your mind is clear. Getting to bed early and starting early works for some. Another approach is to head into the office early or bring lunch and focus while the office is empty. My preference is to work very early or late at night when things are calm and quiet.

4. Reward yourself for completing part or all of a project. It's amazing what you will be able to do when there is a carrot hanging at the end of the stick. Carve out

time to do whatever you love doing only after completing a measurable chunk of whatever project you are on. It can be as simple as going for a treat, run, a bike ride, or a trip to the movies. Rig the game by inviting someone to join you in the fun activity. This way there will be a degree of accountability to help you stay focused.

5. Allow time to wrap work up. One of the most powerful techniques for completing projects is what I call sub-solving. By allowing time to clean up a project in progress then outline the questions and next steps, you set the wheels in motion in the subconscious to work on it.

Completing creative projects can be compared to rolling a 100-pound boulder. Well over half the energy required to get the rock moving is spent getting it started. By posing the questions for next steps during the wrap up process you keep the rock rolling and ready for another push when you come back to it. It works. Try it. This trick will keep projects moving while you are doing other things. This process is amazing, once you see how great this works you will do it naturally.

6. Some people need to schedule time to work on things. I've found too much work planning feels forced and gives the inner-critic a chance to stir up the dreadful procrastination goo. My policy (when possible) has been to get the pieces in place by wrapping up with questions, then forget about it and go about my business. Let things percolate. Then without planning, spontaneously get back to it when the time is right.

7. Remember that you only have so much energy in a given amount of time. Tension fatigue is real. Scale your to-do list expectations to a manageable level. To do good work, find ways to manage feeling overwhelmed and distracted, because that is going to happen.

Rig the game by taking on challenges you can win. Recognize and accept that your mind is trained to seek novelty. Impulse control is power. Relax into putting your attention on intentions, visualize successful results, do the work, then let it go.

All of these techniques are the food that fuels subconscious scripts, where the creative heavy lifting takes place. This process opens access to ideas beyond your personal experience. It may be hard to believe, but a simple leap of faith can open up doors beyond your wildest dreams.

Coming out of the shadows of procrastination feels good. When you work this policy, you'll find yourself completing creative projects big and small like a pro. It is empowering to get things done and downtime becomes more relaxing knowing you have accomplished something.

~~~

It may sound silly to think of having a policy for fun, but in researching this book, I repeatedly heard interviewees say they felt like they were not having enough fun. After taking care of responsibilities I kept hearing that having fun was left for last and too often forgotten.

Fun is the ultimate expression of creativity. Fun activities are the rich reward in a life being well lived. Everybody will have different definitions of play. The skill is in making the time and taking the initiative to get out and live.

Playtime is a need that has been proven to lower anxiety, stress, and blood pressure. Time flies and memories are made when lost in the enjoyment of people, places, activities, and things.

Learning to have genuine fun and finding playful activities nurtures your inner child, calms anxiety and opens doors to the true-you. Playing is a natural relaxer and mood enhancer. I'd like to see more doctors prescribing Frisbee instead of pills.

Fun is where you find it. What was fun as a kid or teen? What anticipations get you jumping out of bed in the morning? Try looking for opportunities to add some fun in while taking care of obligations. Try new things and make time for unstructured activities. Taking care of yourself demands that you are having enough fun.

~~~

Creativity is driven by knowing that there is always a better way. It can be small improvements or a completely new approach. Your way of doing things is an opportunity to shine. Build on existing approaches or combine ideas to create new solutions.

The subconscious creative channels don't respond to effort and energy the same way most challenges in the material world do. In the material world, the harder you work, the longer you stay at it, the more results you (sometimes) get.

When it comes to putting your creative powers to work, find a starting spot, gather information, focus, ask for guidance, then let intuition drive. Break the pieces of a problem into "*how to*" questions, then be patient. If you have followed the steps and are ready to capture ideas when they appear, you've done all you can do. Relax and let the creativity flow.

Here are some creativity policies that seem to work well:
- Do your best without the need for perfection or approval.
- Make playing with friends a priority.
- Maintain the brain by challenging it regularly.
- Play a musical instrument, games, puzzles, etc.

Creativity Maxims:
Different strokes for different folks.
As we seek, so shall we find.
Variety is the spice of life.
A journey of a thousand miles begins with a single step.
Creativity Affirmation – Repeated in present tense with emotional feeling.
I seek creative solutions. </> I find excellent answers.

> **Creativity PPRC**– Do you have creative outlets that you are passionate about?
Satisfaction Scale: 1: Never 2: Low 3-4: Occasional 5-6: Semi-Regular 7-8: Regular 9-10: Complete
_____ Play/Recreation - Factors: fun, groups, non goal-oriented activities, other
_____ Challenged - Factors: work/interests/hobbies, willingness to exit comfort zone?
_____ Art/Music - Factors: make/listen/appreciate, be inspired by, share, other
_____ Intuition - Factors: dialog inner-fan, trusting, control of fears, other
_____ Nature - Factors: have ways to escape/appreciate, travel, camping, ski, other
Score: _____ Grade: _____ Notes: _____
Creativity Pillar Grading: 5-20: D (weak, get moving) / 21-30: C (fragile, keep moving) / 31-40: B (good, but could be better) / 41-50: A (celebrate, strong, doing good, help others, aim for stronger)

Wisewords: *"Imagination is more important than knowledge"* ~Albert Einstein

> Activity: Journey Journal

Keeping a journal is quality get-to-know-yourself time. It is a place where thoughts and feelings are recorded so they can evolve into a conscious awareness you can use to make real progress. Where do you want to be a year from now? In five years? Don't wait, claim it. Journaling helps build mindful awareness into a plan and a path forward.

It's so easy to let life slip by and forget the lessons. Journaling captures lots of memories and useful information that would otherwise be lost to the sands of time. By failing to note (and learn from) thoughts, feelings and the experience of what actually happened, some painful lessons keep repeating. Journaling delivers useful insight.

This is a two-part activity. The first part involves outlining annual goals and priorities. There is a PDF outline for this at PolicyPillars.com.

The second part can be done along with the annual planner or by itself. It is a quick and easy way to build up self-awareness and insight. It can be done in a notebook, on the computer or phone.

The entries do not have to be long or profound, they just have to add meaning to your pillars. Start by simply asking, how do I feel today? What are my current concerns, hopes and priorities? The answers will reveal what is working and what needs attention.

Try adding notes in the morning after meditating as part of the waking up process. Or get to it early in the day before the mind becomes cluttered. Put down impressions and memories of the day, or days just passed. Make entries that bring awareness to the actions, events, people, and places that trigger insight or gratitude. Then look toward the coming days and note how things could unfold.

~~~

This activity bridges the continuity of time, delivering a broader awareness to conscious living. Getting in the habit of spotting gratitude and mapping days brings more awareness to everything. Converting thoughts and experiences into notes helps cement observations into knowingness.

Life comes quickly. It helps to be aware and awake of needs to seize the moments that matter. Making time to note what is happening helps build the savoring muscle, making it quicker at recognizing win-list items. Everything from a good meal, a friendly interaction, some success, scenery, anything meaningful can be noted. Things that do and don't go well can be captured and learned from.

~~~

The simple act of keeping a journal reminds you to be on the lookout for the day's highlights. Knowing that the journal is waiting helps to pay attention rather than mindlessly flowing through the day. This helps connect the dots, raise awareness, and make lasting mental connections. These connections put the past in perspective, bring meaning to the present, and round out policies that prepare for the future. Even if you never go back to read the journal entries, the mental connections are set and working for you.

Keying or speaking journal entries via voice-to-text into the smartphone notes app works great. Do it while in line, stuck in traffic, each morning or evening, but do it daily. Saving it in the cloud allows handy access from phone, desktop, or tablet while keeping the journal backed up.

Actually speaking notes into your phone is not always convenient, so keep a pen and paper handy or tiny voice recorder to capture the moment, then sit down later and make your journal entry.

To keep things cooking, try putting these four questions at the top of the journal then answer them regularly:

1. How do I feel right now? What's going on?

2. How was last night/yesterday/past couple of days? With who? Grateful for?

3. What's coming up? (Prepared? How could it go?) What's on the Win-list?

4. How can I help others today? In the days coming?

~~~

Another approach to the Journey Journal can be done using pictures. Research shows when you pause to take photos of people, places, events, food, whatever, you are immersed in the savoring experience. You actually see the world more clearly when taking photos by looking for things to hang onto. By being engaged, you tend to enjoy it more. Taking photos directs attention to what heightens the pleasure and experience.

The photo/video journal is a place to capture things as they are happening. It helps one stay alert and aware of big and little incidents alike as they become pieces to the puzzle. It is also a place to simply stash grateful memories in a savoring bucket.

Reliving the moments alone and with others is the fun part. Have the computer read the journal aloud; it's quite entertaining. Share insights with friends and family. Print and share the snaps of magic moments. Regularly drop favorite pictures into the computer screensaver folder. Letting memories scroll across the computer or television screen is a lot of fun to watch while reinforcing a sense of purpose, place, and connection. Enjoying and sharing photographs/videos is an easy way to raise the average of life experience.

Wisewords: *"It's the journey that teaches you a lot about your destination."* ~Drake

3. Dreams with Deadlines

Changing lifestyle or habits just because you think you should, or because someone else thinks you should, is never enough. No matter how much you *'think'* you want something or feel obligated to do it, it always comes back to how that something will make you feel. If the goal is not going to feel good, even if you think you are supposed to do something, the odds are against you.

Contrary to popular belief, research shows the primary human drive is not the pursuit of pleasure but rather doing what we find meaningful. Framing goals through the lens of how good they are going to make you feel is rigging the game for success.

~~~

Small goals are usually pretty easy to reach if the rewards are obvious. With big, challenging goals, the reward can seem elusive or too far off to feel real. The inner-critic ego nags away in the subconscious, seducing you into thinking everything is just fine the way it is, even when you know differently. Breaking the goal into smaller steps and keeping the feeling of accomplishment in mind helps drive the emotional energy needed to keep moving forward.

~~~

There are two types of goal drivers: extrinsic and intrinsic. Extrinsic *"outer"* motivation refers to appearances and things like wealth, status, or fame. These rewards deliver short-term satisfaction, but typically leave you wanting more right away. Extrinsic material aspirations are associated with unrealistic idealism, narcissism, anxiety, and depression. This personality type, myself included, is good at achieving goals but often pick the wrong things to strive for. I've come to believe depression and anxiety are more about being a disappointed idealist than any chemical imbalance issues.

It's natural to be drawn to shiny object materialism, but these are mere trinkets compared to inner peace. Living in an extrinsic-driven material media reality can lead to some crazy unrealistic expectations and idealizations. Understanding the source of motivations helps deliver some control over them.

Extrinsic goal examples:

· Learning to play guitar to meet girls.

· Taking a job or choosing a career just for the money.

· Buying a yacht as a status symbol.

· Getting good grades so your parents will buy you something.

Intrinsic *'inner"* motivations on the other hand describe how things feel like personal growth, close relationships, and physical health. Intrinsic motivations are simple and pure. These are driven by an interest or enjoyment in the process of achieving something in and of itself. They come from a place of having nothing to prove and nobody to impress. In general, people who pick intrinsic policies over materialism tend to have more vitality and higher self-esteem. Some intrinsic goal examples include:

· Learning to play guitar because you enjoy music.

· Going to school because you want to learn.

· Taking a job just because it feels right.

· Buying a yacht to share your love of sailing with family and friends.

· Getting good grades because you can.

When you let go of extrinsic ambitions to acquire things or control situations, or any expectation of actually being able change the world, what are you left with? The desire and capacity to love things as they are, enjoy life and help others do the same.

It's not about getting things done because there will always be more to do. It's not about easing guilt or seeking external approval, status, or recognition; those will come and go. It's more about getting things done because you need to and can do them. To do things because they serve your soul, feel right, and are necessary.

It boils down to the source of motivation and how to position desires in your mind. Pursuing goals with intrinsic motivations offers better odds of successfully delivering lasting happiness and satisfaction. Choosing which goals to pursue is the highest form of wisdom.

Wisewords: *"A goal is a dream that has an ending."* ~Duke Ellington

≈ BeSMART Goals

Having goals as policies is more about designing a process than finding a destination. Believing in the ability to steer your life path intentionally releases tremendous emotional power and is a cornerstone of emotional well-being. Adding genuine intrinsic meaning blazes the path to genuine progress. It breeds a confidence and tenacity in the face of stress or challenges. If you feel it, you can heal it! Building in a desire to be of service to others will stoke the emotional energy even further.

One proven logical approach for shaping goals is the SMART model, (Specific, Measurable, Action-oriented, Realistic, and Timely). This is a solid framework to get desires clear, but SMART goals lack two critical components needed for success: (B) belief and (e) emotional fire. Add these fundamental ingredients and you get BeSMART goals.

By bringing belief and emotion into the equation, you empower logical thinking design with emotional feeling energy. Together they create a possibility stew. Nobody captured this concept better than Napoleon Hill when he said *"What the mind can conceive and believe, it can achieve."* in his 1939 classic, *Think and Grow Rich*. Put some heat on that stew and you can cook up just about anything.

Life situations tend to change over time. Framing a BeSMART path to the things you need puts both the conscious and subconscious mind to work. They adapt to the changes that are sure to come and deliver hopeful energy, keeping things moving in the right direction. Try these 7 steps to making BeSMART goals:

1. Put your specific, realistic goals in writing.

2. Divide each big goal into smaller, reachable steps.

3. Make a list of potential obstacles and brainstorm ways around them.

4. Enlist the help of others.

5. Attach a STRONG emotional charge. Fall in love with the feeling of success.

6. Use fear to motivate action, but don't fear failure.

7. Reward yourself each step of the way.

Sounds simple? It is. Easy? You bet. Then why are ninety percent of New Year's resolutions forgotten within a week? Because roadblocks like these are real:

· You don't truly believe you can do it.

· You haven't broken goals down to small enough steps.

· Fear of failure keeps you from actually trying.

One way to break through roadblocks is to put deadlines on your dreams by building Ulysses Contracts. These one-page tools marry intentions to action. They define a policy under construction then build momentum toward authentic change. It takes time. We overestimate what we can accomplish quickly and underestimate what we can become in time. Small steps always lead to progress. A series of steps creates a pattern. The new pattern feels good and takes over. Before you know it, you're there!

Personal intention is a powerful tool that can be supercharged with the help of others. There are many approaches to harnessing group prayer. One technique I've worked with is detailed in the book "The Power of Eight" by Lynn McTaggert. Over 20 years Ms. McTaggert conducted rigorous scientific research on group intention and proved beyond any doubt that shared intention can produce important changes on our physical and mental world. She boiled the approach down to some easy to follow steps that I have personally witnessed change lives. She also detailed the 'intender effect' showing how helping others helps ourselves. Exciting stuff. See the PPI website for a free download of the worksheet we have used in our local group.

~~~

Decision overload and feeling overwhelmed are also problems a lot of us face when making goals. Sometimes it's hard to know what to focus on. Modern living in a marketing-based society presents a ton of daily choices. Cognitive psychologists have determined that it takes a similar amount of energy to decide which toothpaste to buy as it does to pick a book to read. Obviously one choice deserves more attention than the other, but without mindful awareness the brain does not know the difference.

When you stop trying to change, fix or solve the world's problems but rather focus on loving life as it is, one can relax into the appreciation zone. This clarity and release of results or control eases the feeling of being overwhelmed. Just as Clint Eastwood said, *"A man's got to know his limitations."* Acceptance of limits shifts the perception of time from scarcity to abundant yet valuable.

Figuring out goals on relationships, career, investments, and education are all important decisions that are easy to ignore and put off. Life is busy; there is no way to pay close attention to everything. Reframing goals as manageable policies helps quiet the inner-critic to focus on filling in the important needs.

If you were to be offered one million dollars today, or a penny today and then double that amount every day for a month, which would you take? That one shiny penny would grow to $10,737,418.24 in thirty short days! Baby steps get you places. Keep your goals manageable, positive, emotionally charged, in the present tense and they will be working for you. Here are eight tips to ensuring BeSMART goal success:

1. Keep expectations realistic.

2. Ignore the inner-critic.

3. Work inside out from intrinsic motivations.

4. Visualize the sight, smell, touch, sounds, and feeling of success.

5. Take action every day without taking on too much.

6. When setbacks happen, declare a breakdown, ask why, regroup, and move on.

7. Stay flexible and fluid. Allow goals to redefine themselves.

8. Focus on building your personal park.

Research shows that setting small achievable goals builds confidence based on competence. Stringing together a series of small wins leads to big changes. BeSmart goals put you in front of decisions and rig the game for success.

Wisewords: *"If at first you do succeed, try something harder."* ~Ann Landers

≈ Beyond Goals to Policy

If BeSMART goals are the destination, personal policies are the map. Goals always start with the best intentions, logical thinking, or the hope for some reward. They whisper sweet dreams and promises of the new you to get motivated, but often let you down hard the minute they go unfulfilled. Resolutions come and go. This motivation and defeat cycle gnaws away at self-image to a point where ego quits trying.

A goal without a plan is a daydream. As mere mortals, we have a limited amount of time, energy, and willpower, so planning is essential. The ideal of a fresh start, a whole new you, is enticing, but unrealistic. Love it or not, you are who you are now. Change is possible, but it will be a process, not a destination.

Policies are used to solve problems. Goals are the building blocks to a personal policy set. They gather strategies and build motivation to push through resistance while building resilience. They turn priorities into plans.

This process goes beyond hoping for good things to happen. It adds structure, strategy, the guidance of feelings, and the energy of genuine hope to create and maintain the new patterns you want. Just as governments, industries and organizations use policies to coordinate the actions and activities of their many parts, people can use them to help manage the complexities of personal growth.

~~~

Policy setting begins with keeping your ideal state of being in mind and learning from what works. Visualize outcomes, situations, and scenarios, then work from the bottom up detailing the steps to get there. Step back and observe yourself in the reality zone. Make the win-list real. Only from the outside can you see the center.

One way to test goals to see if they fit into your personal policies is to ask yourself the 'five fives': Will this plan serve me and move me toward my best self in five minutes? Five days? Five weeks? Five months and five years? If the answers are yes, then do it, learn it, be it. But just making policies is not enough. Change takes time. There will be setbacks. You must go in committed to recommitting.

Many daydreams can become reality by employing the power of clear intention (goals), some planning (strategy), and choices (actions) all fueled with emotion. Just as companies have mission statements, personal policies help you stay on track. Getting clear about policies is a process of examining needs, picturing your park, creating expectations and taking action.

Just as the purpose of the universe is to expand, our purpose may simply be to become our best authentic self while helping others do the same. The personal policies you define can draw upon all you are, all you have done, all you know, and all you hope for. They are the secret sauce to your burger.

Wisewords: *"Our goals can only be reached through a vehicle of a plan, in which we must fervently believe, and upon which we must vigorously act. There is no other route to success."* ~Pablo Picasso

≈ Making Policy Personal

Ever made a promise to a friend? When you make a promise to yourself, it's called a policy. Policies are agreements with yourself, good ideas paired with a plan. Everyone is faced with choices: Date the boy, marry the girl, go to school, take the job, how to manage money, live healthy and have some fun. Sometimes we have to choose compromise between two things we really want such as attraction and compatibility. How you make these decisions is the art of personal policy-making.

The term policy is typically applied to government, corporate, and nonprofit groups. Presidential executive orders, company procedures, and parliamentary rules of order are all examples of policy in organizations. Personnel handbooks direct the best behavior of employees. Policy differs from rules or law, which are strict ways to compel or prohibit behaviors. Policies offer flexibility by focusing on outcomes more than the process.

I've found personal policy-making to be the artful science of mindful living. It is the crystallization of unique desires into smart plans with manageable steps. Policies paired with personal growth techniques have been a rope pulling me through transitions into the future. This is one technique that can unite experiences, studies, hopes, dreams, and desires. I've found that if you work for them they will work for you. What is personal policy? The dictionary definition is revealing:

pol·i·cy (noun)

1. A program of actions adopted by an individual, group, or government. The set of principles which guides how choices are made and actions are based.

2. Shrewdness or prudence, especially in the pursuit of goals or a particular course of action.

Policies are common sense, flexible guidelines that adapt to your uniqueness and an ever-changing world. These ideas act as boundaries keeping you on the right track. Defining personal policies delivers guidance on what is right for you, and the power to say no to the things that don't work. They deliver the strength to walk forward confidently and consistently into the unknown toward highest and best purposes. Once we see our boundaries, there are none.

Policies serve organizations and can serve you as well. These may seem simple like New Year's resolutions but are really much more than that. They build from the inside out to leverage desire and wisdom into decisions and action. They are strategies and techniques based on experience and common sense. They combine logical thinking with emotional feeling to create the conditions for authentic change.

There are an infinite number of personal policies; you choose or tailor them to your specific situations and needs. Policies can come from many sources but all trace their roots back to proven wisdom on what has worked (or not worked) for you and others. You can think of personal policies as hopes, strategies, principles and expectations all whipped into one.

~~~

Personal policy-making is recognition that there is always a better way, and that all puzzles have solutions. They relieve some of the pressure to conform or perform to the norm by recognizing and celebrating the fact that though all is connected, all are unique. They support becoming your best possible self. All policies are built on three core principles:

1. Bits of wisdom and codes of conduct based on personal experience and/or the know-how of others.

2. Guidelines, not rules. They adapt to exceptions, transitions, and changing priorities over time.

3. Personal and tailored to your unique situations and circumstances.

Policies ease the process of trial and error by giving you maps and tools to bring plans together. Like the little grooves cut in on the side of a road to wake up tired drivers, policies keep you out of trouble and moving forward down the road of life. They help you find natural solutions to the many options we all have. Defining your pillars and putting effort into updating policies when needed is like having a personal coach working for you all the time. For example here are a few of mine:

Health Pillar

· Eat light and healthy at least four days a week. Cook more.

· Be in bed with the radio off by midnight five days a week.

· Find ways to accept myself and manage stress without addictions.

· Exercise vigorously four days every week.

Relationships Pillar

· Make relationship-building a priority.

· Look for opportunities to support and help others.

Resources Pillar

· Save money and invest for the future.

· Live with a light footprint, conserve, and never pollute.

· Allow enough time to get ready and get where I need to be.

· Selectively keep news and media intake to a comfortable limit.

Responsibility Pillar

· Don't start something unless I honestly believe I can finish it.

· Do my very best work with all projects I do decide to take on.

· Take the time needed to make decisions I will not regret.

· Live with integrity. When I fail, make amends right away.

Creativity/Fun Pillar

· Make time to research or write (nearly) every day.

· Regularly allow free time to play, relax, and explore.

As obvious as these are, deciding to make these policies priorities has paid huge ongoing dividends. Some didn't require much effort to make them a habit. I've needed help with others.

Policies are deeper and more thought out than resolutions. They build out from core needs and desires mapping the path ahead. They help define oneself and help others understand where you are coming from. They are ropes to the future, guiding and pulling forward.

~~~

One example of a simple yet powerful choice is my sleep policy. I'm a night owl, always have been. I like that quiet time to myself and don't want to waste it on sleep. Typically, I would stay up until 2 AM most nights, just barely squeezing in six or seven hours of sleep. After watching some documentaries and reading up on the importance and nature of sleep, it became obvious I was doing it wrong. Even though I was getting enough hours, research showed our natural circadian cycles provide the deep sleep we need between 10 PM and 6 AM. This makes sense as humans have followed the patterns of the sun for eons.

I used to wake up in a sour mood and just believed it was a typical morning thing. As it turns out, these were my emotions, mind and body telling me, for decades, that something was out of balance. I ignored that message, rationalized unhealthy behavior, and deeply regret it. I feel sorry for all the people over the years that had to be around me in the morning. Please accept my apologies.

Since I have updated my sleep strategy, the benefits have been enormous. Not only am I feeling healthier in general, looking more rested, my energy, attitude, and level of motivation have soared. These days, more often than not, I wake up in a good mood, energized, rested, and ready to appreciate another day. I'm getting a ton of good work done in the mornings and feeling more in control of my time.

Needs can be ignored for a long time but what we resist persists. Once you feel the benefits, policies become an easy habit.

Wisewords: *"Honesty is the best policy."* ~Benjamin Franklin

≈ Benefits of Personal Policies

How many times have you thought, "*I wish I knew then what I know now*?" Learning through experience works, but is hard and slow. Most of the answers to life's questions are out there. Policies build on proven wisdom to help piece together beliefs and priorities.

Policies help you snap your fingers and wake up. They become an internal compass - even when the path forward is not clearly marked, they keep you pointed in the right direction. They make choices easier while unleashing the power of positive expectation. Declared policies help others understand and support you.

There have been some critical transitions and lots of small but important decisions where I wish I had the guidance of good policy on my side. Dropping out of school, relocating away from friends, changing careers - all important crossroads. Choices big and small often have a major impact on life, and alter the course of the years to come.

Looking back, lots of decisions have been made without much thought. I just went along with what was happening. The experiences have made me who I am, but brought along some limiting beliefs, stress and regrets.

I have come to trust that stress and regret are wasted energy. All the worrying in the world will not change the past, only ruin the present. You are just giving your power away.

Mindfulness taps the past to be present with a positive expectation of the future. Just as with the placebo effect, where belief cures illness, policies can "*cure*" fear of uncertainty enough to keep moving.

The Serenity Prayer is the best policy ever - a stress and worry eraser: "*God* (or whatever power you believe in), *grant me the serenity to accept the things I cannot change, the courage to change the things I can, and the wisdom to know the difference.*" Policies help you know the difference.

~~~

A simple example of how policies can work on many levels is the posture policy. Everyone knows that upright posture is good for the back, but may not know how it can affect attitude as well.

Several years ago I was experiencing regular back pain, which left me feeling tired and old. Though I hit the gym regularly, my body was telling me something was wrong. I searched the web for information and found the number one approach to back wellness was to maintain a good posture.

The various sources suggested exercising the transverse abdominal oblique muscles by holding in the stomach (without holding the breath). This behavior of drawing the belly button into your spine is also referred to as activating your core. It is done by standing or sitting straight, exhaling, and drawing the navel to the spine. This sounded simple enough and I believed this would work for me. My aim became to see how long I could maintain awareness to hold a healthy posture each day.

This is how personal policies work, when a strategy is so obvious there is no choice but to try living it. Staying in pain was not an option. I had a simple plan built on common wisdom with good odds of working. Reminders went up in places where I spent a lot of time (at work, on the couch, the car, the motorcycle). I built a stand-up desk at the office, started yoga and swimming at the gym, trusted and expected that the policy would work, and it did.

Within a couple of months, the back pain was gone and has stayed away. The choice to adopt some new behaviors came from a belief in what has worked for others and reinforced by what it has done for me.

This example demonstrates how policies can help. I had a problem, a painful one that was interfering with every part of life. I had been to doctors and trainers, tried inversion machines and had spent a lot of time in the jacuzzi. Nothing was helping and painkillers were not an option. After seeking a proven solution, a plausible answer appeared; trial brought success.

As the habit took hold, it seemed things were going better at work and in social life too. I discovered studies that showed how posture projects an expectation of success, leading to positive outcomes. Holding an upright chest out in the "*looking big*" core posture brings interest and respect. Just as we feel sad when fake crying or feel better when fake smiling, good posture opens doors and supports self-esteem.

The mind-body connection is undeniable. Feeling good is great and better relationships have been a nice bonus.

Policies have helped me lose weight, mend some broken relationships, quit smoking, fix some rotten teeth, change careers, get finances in order, make some investments, move to the coast, and much more. I had known for a long time that I needed to make these changes. I had made resolutions and tried, but wishful thinking alone was not enough. It took strategies for overcoming obstacles, personal growth techniques and persistence to bring the ideas into action.

Like spiritual belief, religion, science, and philosophy, policies are a way to set expectations, help make sense of, and organize, the world around us. They prepare you for everyday living and those inevitable moments when life is turned upside down. Once yours are established, you will know more about yourself. Once shared others will know more about who you are, where you are coming from, and what they expect from you.

I like to think of policies as self-service; by taking care of yourself you can be of service to others. Adopting a policy-based approach to personal growth can be a huge step in your evolution as a human being.

Wisewords: *"Simplicity is the ultimate sophistication."* ~Leonardo da Vinci

≈ Developing Personal Policies

Making policy is about waking up to new dimensions of yourself. These aspects of the true-you are already there, just waiting to be recognized and developed. For whatever reason — perceived need of something from the outside, fear, stress, lack of knowledge — they are trapped inside. Policies recognize that it's not the outside people, situations or things that free or paralyze you, it's your thoughts about them that rule.

A well-cultivated life is regularly pruned with personal policies so as to take on the shape we desire. The process of identifying, visioning, and building policy strategies pulls you into the person you know you are. Slowing down long enough to ask for guidance allows you to be vulnerable enough to take action on the areas you can improve while being relaxed enough to accept being exactly as you are here and now.

There is no one set of policies for everybody; yours will be different than mine. Defining and designing them is a completely individual experience. No two people will approach it exactly the same way.

Policies work for you when you put the work into tailoring them to meet needs, then build up enough energy to push through resistance. When you allow resistance to rule existence it drains persistence.

Defining positive expectations backed up by manageable actions is not a passive exercise. It demands honest self-evaluation, time, and willingness to use the tools of transformation. This process puts you in charge of deciding what is important, then guides how to get there. Here are five ideas on how to pick policies:

1. Take a careful look at the nature and aim of your life. Ask: Is this my best possible self? What's missing? What are my true needs? What are my priorities? How do I want to feel inside? How do I want to show up to others?

2. Review how your life is organized. Look clearly and honestly at what you think about and spend your time doing, then form win-lists based on what you want to have happening. (See activity: Build a Win-List, below.)

3. Be a policy detective. Learn to spot other people's policies that could work for you. Go to seminars and study books, audio, or video for clues and nuggets that fit into your evolving life manual. Capture these in Ulysses Contracts (appendix) then invest energy into the process.

4. When policy initiatives affect others, sit down with them and describe how you see things changing, and what you hope to see happen. Avoid generalities. Make your vision specific, measurable, attainable, and emotional. Add a time element, and make sure you have clearly communicated expectations. Ask friends and associates for feedback. Listen.

5. Roll all your tools and techniques into win-list thinking. Have fun putting the best you center stage in thoughts. Stay conscious of all five pillars while continuing to discover, re-evaluate, and reassess policies. Commit to recommitting. Be willing to pivot, modify, or delete policies that aren't working.

At this point it's easy to stop and say, "*Yes, but...I can't, won't, don't know how...*," these excuses are all fear-fueled inner-critic ANT worrying about a future that has yet to materialize. Stop it.

Wisewords: *"You were born to win, but to be a winner, you must plan to win, prepare to win, and expect to win."* ~Zig Ziglar

> Activity: Build a Win-List

Detailing win-lists can be one of the most clarifying and empowering activities on the road to self-discovery. The idea is simple: what you stay mindful of and look for is what you see. Create a list for each of the five pillars on what is good now and what you want the future you to have going on. Use these details to stream movie trailers in your mind starring the true, self-aware, grateful, satisfied you. Repeat.

Think backward to note feelings, feedback from others and signs of success. Think forward to snippets of the action as if you are already there, a preview of life's coming attractions. This will act as a magnet through the law of attraction to bend reality and pull those situations together. What you focus on is what you get. That's it. There are a couple of things to keep in mind, though:

1. Your present self cannot clearly visualize past stress, fears, prejudices, and dusty beliefs unless you give it permission. Find faith in the future. While forging your win-list, focus on intrinsic meaning instead of pleasure. Pleasure is a self-centered activity, a recreational, sensual gratification that can be grand, but cannot last. Meaning is a core emotion that feels good and creates mental connections that last. What syncs in the brain links in the brain. The bonus is that as you seek meaning, there will be much pleasure along the way.

2. Shift gears between the present, near-term, medium, and distant future modes. Looking toward next year paints the broad strokes. Visualizing best-case scenarios for this afternoon, evening, or weekend fills in details now so they are there when needed. Focus on things already on the calendar. The job, the meeting, the date, outing, gathering, all fertile ground to plant on. Zoom out. What do you have going on in five years? Ten years? The elderly you?

For each pillar, detail the win-list with notes of what's worked, what's working, and what will be. Add notes when successes happen or when others share positive feedback. Add visualizations with an emotional punch, what does the true-you lifestyle look and feel like? What's going on? Who's there?

This rooted fantasizing is fun but structured with intention. Add details. Let the stories run and play out. Make it a fun go-to daydream channel. Here are some examples to let your mind run wild with:

Health: Enjoying exercise, eating delicious nutritious meals, looking & feeling great.
Relationships: Enjoying rich relationships, shared interests, and interdependence.
Resources: Experience yourself making smart use of time, energy, and money.
Responsibility: Feeling the results of great choices. Being needed.
Creativity/fun: Reflecting on wins, successes, creative solutions, and good times.
For others: Picturing good things for others triggers energy supporting your needs.

Add sensation by triggering emotions, touch, smells, and sounds of win-list events. Feel great about things that have not happened yet. Laugh out loud over jokes yet to be told. See the bank account and calendar full. Feel the chill as you pull leftovers out of the fridge from meals yet to be made.

As inner-critic ANTs creep in, just let them go by and refocus. I don't mean to make this sound easy, because it's not. It's natural to focus on what's wrong, broken, or missing. The win-list is about training the mind to savor the present while building a vision for an outstanding future. When in doubt, go to gratitude.

~~~

Make note of success as it unfolds. Focus on what's next then let the fun future-you thoughts go. Don't obsess or cement expectations. Guide the visualizations to believable stopping points, then release. Drop it like a rope into a well. Visualize it dissolving into the universe. Then forget it. This broadcasts the energetic feeling, making connections, attracting what you need.

You will feel calmer, happier, and physically better as the thoughts take form. Seeing life this way patterns the progress. Personally, it took about three weeks of gently reminding myself to shift thoughts of worry or fixing things into visualizing win-list pillars. It has become a natural instinct, a go-to habit while relaxing, in line, driving, swimming, off and on all day long, everyday.

This exercise continues to offer amazing results. Usually things go much better than I had hoped for, often in unexpected ways. Raising awareness of what you're looking for and want to have going on tickles the subconscious to guide priorities, choices, actions, and activities into making those things happen.

Awareness triggers real-time intention to do the right things or ask the right questions at the right time instead of later thinking back on what you could have said or done differently. As things come to be, stop, give thanks, and realize how powerful you are.

This is a trusted technique for preparing the mind to pay attention to intuition and synchronicity. It's funny, if you give hope some structure, things always work out exactly as needed.

~~~

Use the pillars as a mental checklist, then expect that the thoughts you need at that moment will appear. Sometimes I'll sit in nature or meditate across the pillars, setting realistic expectations while picturing positive outcomes. Or I'll just sit at my desk and go through the pillars in my head. As thoughts crystallize, I'll stop to send an email, make a call, take notes, book a date, do the things that the visualizations triggered.

One delicious example of how this works showed up in a health policy to eat better. I love tasty food and have been lucky to be surrounded by some great cooks over the years, but never learned much about preparing food for myself. As I started visualizing homemade meals on my table, things started to happen on the shopping list and in the kitchen. Quick searches for simple recipes turned into great meals. Confidence and skills have grown. Tasty, healthy food is becoming the norm.

Play with adding emotional detail to the recurring threads. Picture, daydream, and meditate on new rhythms instead of routines. The win-list rigs the game by filling in details of the future you instead of mindlessly going with the flow. It's not rocket science — repetition builds recognition. Paint pretty life landscapes in your mind, add detail from the perspective of what you want as already having happened. Release. Repeat.

When negativity, fears, or old beliefs get in the way, say, "*Go away until you have something new to say.*" They never do and soon the limits will fall away. To help win-list thinking become a habit make some Ulysses Contracts to give visualizations more structure. Use them to capture detail, emotion, expectations, and rewards for each pillar. As each pillar feels strong, drill down and dig deeper. Once you see it you can be it.

Win-List insights & ideas:

Health: _____

_____

_____

_____

Relationships: _____

_____

_____

_____

Resources: _____

_____

_____

_____

Responsibility: _____

_____

_____

_____

Creativity/fun: _____

_____

_____

_____

Wisewords: *"The harder you work... and visualize something, the luckier you get."*
~ Seal

≈ Coach U

Most of us know what needs to be done to improve our life situation, but may not know the steps or have the skills to achieve them. You can try to fake it until you make it. Or find a guide.

Top achievers all have coaches. Even with everything they have accomplished, most know they have more inside to give. A coach focuses priorities, encourages action even when the going gets tough, then offers feedback. That's how we learn.

A coach never trains two individuals the same way. A good coach knows about your past, is aware of your present situation, is clear on what you are capable of, and pushes you to get there. Coaches give you the tools for success and hold you accountable through the process. They teach consistency over intensity, aiming to make growth a habit. We all need a coach. In this case, you are the coach and the climber.

To get your coach on the job, start by tackling some of the smaller things on the win-list. Do you feel disorganized or have piles of paperwork? It is a proven fact that clutter makes us tense and unable to focus on important items. Implementing a get-organized policy can clear the mess and free the mind for deeper thinking. Feeling low in energy? Saddle up to an exercise or Mediterranean diet policy to get back in the groove. Simple policies for each pillar can make a big difference fast.

Small successes build confidence and lay the foundation to strike larger issues. Want to get more control of your resources? Feeling isolated or stuck in relationship ruts? There are common sense policies for each.

Stepping up to your life plan awareness is akin to walking up a staircase, each step climbing higher and closer to the true-you. Visualize the path starting with the Desire (I want). Use awareness to focus on needs. Stop. Look back. Take inventory of accomplishments and all you are grateful for. Bring some personal development to the table for new or upgraded skills. Pull habit and practice together with personal policy. Repeat.

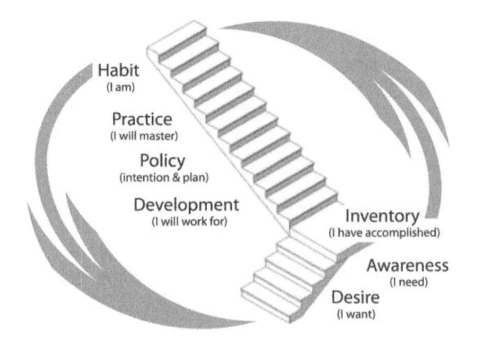

Habit
(I am)

Practice
(I will master)

Policy
(intention & plan)

Development
(I will work for)

Inventory
(I have accomplished)

Awareness
(I need)

Desire
(I want)

There are no shortcuts. Even if you do find a way to skip steps, odds are the pain of falling backwards will be worse than steady climbing.

Accomplishment will spur the coach to ask for more. It's not about speed or destinations. As soon as you get anywhere you are going to want more. The solution to one problem defines the next. Climbing implies progress, balance, patience, and process.

Enjoy the ride. There's only one final destination in life, and personally I'm in no rush to get there.

~~~

To acknowledge the natural order of taking steps forward is to stop fighting and start flowing. As policies are established and become part of daily practice, ego, delusion, fear, and doubt fall away, leaving a clearer view of who you are, what you have to work with, whom you can help, and how to go about thriving.

It has been said that knowledge is power; this is only half true. True power comes from the knowledge that you can gain skills and find resources to improve any situation. Don't let not knowing how stop you from doing anything. Making a habit of learning is the most important investment you can make in yourself. Trust in abilities, then move one step at a time.

Ultimately, it will take focus, willpower, compromise, and time to find your unique path forward. In the game of life, not coaching yourself leads to anxiety and stress. Sitting on the sidelines can deliver a nice view, but that's not where the action is.

Wisewords: *"Dogs have boundless enthusiasm but no sense of shame. I should have a dog as a life coach."* ~Moby

≈ Be a Genius

The definition of a genius includes some predictable stuff: intellectual ability, originality, brilliance, creativity, mathematical aptitude, etc. Mental horsepower is nice, but is rarely an indicator of who will be successful. There are three things far more important to accomplishment than being IQ test smart: mindfulness, practice, and persistence. And all three are completely under your control.

The ability to stay mindful on priorities is a powerful skill. This starts by slowing what the Buddhists refer to as the "*monkey mind*," or the restless and confusing thought parade in the head, long enough to make sense of true intentions and put wisdom to work filling true needs.

Learn to focus by practicing. Start with twenty minutes of uninterrupted focus on something you want to master, turn off the phone, no TV or radio. Focus. Start with a breathing meditation then sit still and stay focused.

Rig the game for success by starting first thing in the morning with meditation and journaling before getting distracted with email or news. To focus later in the day, try having chores, exercise, meals, calls all done. Have a tidy work area and allow some time for your mind to wind down. Light a candle, put on a symphony, make some tea, and do some good work.

The last key totally under your control is persistence. Most of the people we celebrate as geniuses invested massive study and practice before being noticed. Accomplished scientists, athletes, engineers, artists, business people, musicians, and dancers all persisted before making their mark. There is usually at least ten years of work behind every overnight success.

~~~

I once had a boss, Sam P., a great can-do fellow who consistently challenged me to complete big projects. Every afternoon, Sam would dial into his office for an undisturbed hour to focus on one project, his hour of power. I learned quickly that to have a prayer of doing the work I was charged with, several hours of power were needed every day.

Over time, the projects came to life and prospered. Confidence brought more challenges, responsibility, and opportunity. I think of Sam often. He helped me to remember that genius simply meant getting the skills, doing the research, taking the risks, but most importantly, investing the time.

We celebrate people not for their IQ, but for their accomplishments. My guess is that most us want to do some great things in this life. Raising a child or building a business will force you into becoming a genius. It's a good bet that keeping mindful of priorities will make you a genius in your own right. What do you want to accomplish? What turns you on? What do you lose time doing? Whatever it is, why not become a genius at it?

Wisewords: *"Genius is one percent inspiration and ninety-nine percent perspiration."* ~Thomas A. Edison

4. Master of the Universe

Whatever the path of advancement or retreat, every step toward self-discovery is a victory. To become master of your universe is to accept everything as a gift.

Everything knowable is filtered by the brain operating system. These quantum agreements with the inner-fan and critic create a lens of perception on reality.

Different situations, backgrounds, ambitions, and cultures bring flavor to the wisdom of being human, but at the core, we are all the same. To tap inner wisdom is to trust intuition like you would a best friend. Intuition is the guide and policies are your partners.

Intuition, priorities, intentions, actions, and habits all create luck in the Unified Field. Think of habits as your wardrobe. These behaviors define your style, taste, how you see yourself and others see you. How do you look? How would you like to look? Where would you shop for fresh beliefs and once there, what would you buy? Policies are the threads sewing the seams of your habit wardrobe together.

The big changes we all seek will be the result of a series of large and small decisions, choices, and personal style. The new you will be more of an improved you, slightly different in areas that matter, always evolving.

Reality check: the dream of a rapid total transformation, a new you, is a myth. It took time to become the person you are and will take some time to reinvent yourself. All your qualities - good, bad, and neutral - have built up over time, reinforced by people, situations, and ego.

The traits we admire and celebrate - creativity, style, vulnerability, humility, graciousness, confidence, and magnetism - are all constructs of the mind. Nearly every waking moment is spent writing and rewriting life scripts. Use the ideas in this section to spark the art of awareness.

Wisewords: *"Everything is perfect in the universe - even your desire to improve it."*
~Wayne Dyer

≈ The Unified Field

There is a fundamental consciousness and energetic wisdom that unifies the past, present, and future. It connects people, plants, animals, places, planets, and beyond. This wavelength is known by several names: God, Chi, life force, spirit, the soul, collective consciousness, and a hundred others. In this work, I have chosen to work with the concept of the Unified Field, but please call it whatever feels right.

This universal intelligence is available to everyone all the time. It crosses all borders of time, space, language, and culture. Just as a smile or a tear speaks without words, the Unified Field connects and affects us all. The more you pay attention to it, the more it can be employed.

The idea of a Unified Field (UF) was proposed by Albert Einstein. He attempted to unify his general theory of relativity, which explains behavior of the very large (planets, solar systems, universe) with the quantum non-local properties of the very small (atoms, electrons…). It was to be his Theory of Everything.

According to Einstein, this Unified Field drives the physics of the universe; it acts like the invisible force of a magnet, a cosmic Wi-Fi attracting or repelling matter and energy. He felt everything was cosmically 'alive' and that UF is the gel connecting and affecting everything. Einstein was never able to prove his ideas mathematically. Scientists continue to pursue proof of this intelligence behind life patterns, but its workings remain unknown.

~~~

Looking at the physiology of living beings electromagnetically reveals neural pathways that send and receive electric energy across the brain, heart and all the organs. The heart is much more than a muscle. It is the electromagnetic center of our network, providing a feeling of balance to the mind's logic. Strong connections between the two are needed to get the full picture.

Our entire neurological system is a UF antenna capable of giving and receiving guidance from others and beyond. We don't really need to know how it works, just that it does. There is no point in arguing its existence; it defies description and simply is.

This force is powered by a subtle but very real energy working tirelessly below the conscious plane. It connects and guides everything on a quantum level. Just as with gravity, it's something you can't see, but know it's there. While this energy can be felt, it defies precise measure. As a result, its study has been primarily left to spirituality, psychology, and metaphysics.

The UF is strong in the reality zone. It has a balancing effect in the universe, and on our personal world of striving and savoring. Making a policy to cultivate your relationship with this supreme force of nature taps into its power. It's how visualizing a win-list brings dreams into reality.

Think of it as a karmic gel that binds the present to the past and the future. Ancient civilizations across the planet likely used it to build mega-monuments. Churches and spiritual gurus peddle it. Athletes, artists, and musicians play with it. Personal policies help you to remember how to stay on the right side, employ, manage, and flow with it.

There are many ways the Unified Field communicates consciousness in daily activities. When you happen to be looking at someone across the room or in another car and they suddenly pop their head up and look back. The energy of a crowd at sports events and concerts unites all involved. Dancing is a fun way to flirt with UF source energy. A smile almost always brings a smile back. Eighty percent of the Billboard Magazine Top 100 Singles involve a theme of love or romance, strong forces in the UF.

Laughter and crying are interesting examples of this connective energy. No one knows exactly why we find things funny or how tears work in the brain. I believe it is a manifestation of our UF connection. These are ways beyond language that we signal each other that we "*get it*" and agree, or are hurting and need help. Both are contagious and deliver a bonding experience between a few or many people in an instant.

It is also a way to break and release blocked energy. In Buddhism the answer to every question of personal limits is to laugh heartily out loud. But as much as we all love to laugh, we cannot tickle ourselves; it can't be faked.

The UF is without bias, neither supporting or restricting a life path. More like a reflection you get out of it what you put into it. Any intention, expectation or

94

emotion is a conversation with this source. What you think about is what you get. It's psychic physics.

I've heard many artists, musicians, and writers describing their experience with creative work as if the inspiration came from an unknown place, as if they are a channel tuned into a shared source. Writing has proven this to me. I definitely feel an invisible force in the UF has been driving the endless research, writing, and editing. I know these words build on the work of others, pushing the conversation along.

Wisewords: *"Even if there is only one possible unified theory, it is just a set of rules and equations. What is it that breathes fire into the equations and makes a universe for them to describe?"* ~Stephen Hawking

≈ Brain Operating System (B.OS)

How do you know when to upgrade a computer operating system? When it starts slowing down or fails to do what you want when you want. Just imagine if you downloaded new software for your computer and it refused to install all of the updates you were expecting! What if it selectively allowed some or none of the updates on its hard drive based on how the ego chip felt at the moment? I bet many of us would still be in 1985 running WordStar on an x286.

The conundrum is that many of us are trained with left-brain logic to solve problems. While this can work quite well in school or on the job, it's not how thinking naturally works. Our mind runs snippets of code in the core of our creative, emotional right brain. These emotional connections drive beliefs that rule the subconscious scripts driving choices/behaviors/habits. This is why it is impossible to think your way through self-improvement.

To get both sides working properly, you may need to upgrade the Brain Operating System (B.OS). This biocomputer inside the head is programmed full of beliefs, feelings, and thoughts that create reality from a bunch of stories and expectations. It ties the human energetic software through the UF to the hardware of the material world.

~~~

Computer operating systems know when to discard outdated instructions, re-average the balances, install new code, fix old scripts, and create new ones. Humans often don't. Unlike a computer, wildcard ego gets attached to ideas, acts randomly or takes the lazy way out. Personal upgrade alerts in the form of worry or stress will keep popping up until they are addressed. Clicking "*Ignore*" will not make the needs go away.

With out-of-date software we perceive and react in habitual (tired), predictable ways. This narrative lies someplace between accepting reality and complete delusion. It is almost always simplified and often distorted by ego to fit neatly with other scripts already in place. Just like in the *Matrix* movies we have a choice to live in delusion or use knowledge and wisdom to seek personal truth.

96

If our brain is the computer, then the thoughts are the software we run. It's amazing our mental code works as well as it does. We do what we think we are supposed to do and hope for the best. In most situations, this works out okay. Sometimes things go terribly wrong. Thoughts are like traffic, if you run on to the freeway and try to control them you'll get smashed. Putting wise policies to work adds signs and signals to tame the traffic so we can get our software up to date.

Everyone is running different software and we all have unique upgrade needs. Some need to calm down, others will benefit by adding excitement, being more grateful, loving, adventurous, creative, patient, healthy, focusing on improving relationships, growing resources, etc. Whatever will make your mind work better, wherever true needs lie, is where your policies will be found.

Leveraging the wisdom of good policies gets you where you want to be faster and with less stress. Policies can't always eliminate stress, but they can help re-pattern your B.OS response to it.

Research done using virtual reality has shown that the mind can easily be tricked into thinking an emotion is real even when it is not based on reality. Even imagined fear and anxiety triggers harmful biological changes. A finely tuned B.OS knows the difference and invests harmless energy into positive, supportive win-list thoughts while starving negative ones.

To upgrade your mind means to fine-tune the ability to focus on what serves and supports, while weeding out the illusions, people, and predicaments that don't. An ongoing averaging of experience.

~~~

Upgrading the B.OS means releasing sole attachment to serving yourself or any grand expectations that some perfect purpose, person, or position is out there waiting for you. Well-crafted scripts guide you to look for meaning from within. Purpose is simply about doing what you need to do to feel good about yourself. When you have your priorities in order and take care of your business, everything will fall into place.

Updating the mind's software is about overcoming fear and putting consistent effort into personal understanding. It's not a destination or possession but rather a process of positioning yourself in the flow of life. Upgrades help spot the people, actions, and activities that feel right. Elegant mental software also knows how to let things that don't serve you go, freeing up space for the true-you to load and run.

Being open to reality can be scary or stimulating: it's a choice. To resist change is to hold on to the past, to accept change is to let go and get on with it. Just as classic Buddhist examples demonstrate that it's impossible to hold the breath indefinitely or grasp water to stop it from flowing, you can't begin the next chapters of your life while running the last ones over and over. Change can be frightening, but it can also set you free.

~~~

Brain scientists say our operating system lives in the prefrontal cortex and the amygdala, just above and behind your eyes. This "*mind's eye*" is where the complex cognitive behavior of planning, personality, style, decision-making, moderating social behavior, and a bunch of other really important imagination stuff goes on.

This is our experience simulator, the land of the win-list. It's a place where you can picture yourself doing just about anything. It's where you replay future events before they've happened. Picturing an idealized life writes fresh software.

In the mind's eye, thoughts and actions have to balance with reality. It's easy to see yourself in that super situation, with that super person, doing or having that super thing, but it's a dangerous glitch. This is how advertising works.

Marketers have wired us to respond to the emotions of need, greed, fear, and the desire for exclusivity. But it's not healthy to try to synthesize happiness by wishing, wanting, and coveting what others appear to have. Appearances are misleading. Untamed imagination pulls us down fantasy paths that are destined to disappoint.

Think about where your life was at five or ten years ago; odds are a lot has changed. Now ask yourself: did I design these changes? Or did they just kind of happen? Think about where you might be had there been clear priorities, a plan, a vision, and a consistency of purpose over the last decade.

Even if things have gone pretty well, could they have gone even better? Everything is constantly changing and evolving. Identity is really just an accumulation of memories, beliefs and expectations you call yourself. Managing these creates the new you.

Freedom is often as much about appreciating things that don't happen! Make a smart purchase and the car will not break down. Avoid a job or relationship that doesn't feel right and you will be available when the right one does come along. Staying healthy, vital, and connected often involves a lot of glorious non-events.

More and more it seems the best decisions I've made are about not doing or saying things. Not spending time with people I don't really want to, not watching mindless TV, not clicking on links I know won't serve me. The word "*no*" is the most powerful word in any language. You can't say yes if you can't say no.

No sets limits and frees up space. Consider becoming a savvy consumer of life. Saying no to that which no longer serves or supports updates B.OS programming. No creates time and energy to focus on what really matters.

Our mind's computer has infinite storage and is already connected to all wisdom scripts, but you have to command the upgrade. While installing new code you can't continue to function as normal. You have to take a break. Install new scripts with education, meditation, and by spending time with friends and mentors. Exercise, take a vacation, make dinner, nap. Try some of the techniques listed at the PPI website, find others or create your own.

Cleaning up random mental chatter while letting go of self-defeating behaviors is the process of updating mental software. Policies are the quantum agreements between you, your current self, future self, and the inner-fan.

There are no shortcuts to peace of mind. It's about learning to see things clearly in the light of that which supports your best self. This process will require trust, effort, and willpower, but success sneaks up on you.

Wisewords: *"This planet came with a set of instructions, but we seem to have misplaced them. Civilization needs a new operating system."* ~Paul Hawken

≈ Cleaning the Lens

Finding personal truth demands a clear line of sight. The concept of a lens of perception describes how you see the world and the expectations made from what you see. Lenses, by definition, filter the convergence of light or correct defects of vision. They change what is seen. Awareness and acceptance determine how clear or dirty the mind lens will be.

Eastern wisdom says all suffering comes from three dirty thought lens patterns: attraction, aversion, and delusion. Suffering leads to pain when we dwell on things (often beyond our control) through the lens of attraction (wanting things we don't have), aversion (not wanting the things we do have) and delusion (seeing things not as they actually are). In other words, suffering is not from what is, but from wishing and wanting life to be different than it is.

Sometimes the dirt gets so thick we quite literally can't see the things we need. Over time, the muck of tired beliefs and unrealistic expectations builds up, blocking the ability to see yourself in the world clearly. Ignorance, half-truths, judgment, prejudices, taking things personally, false science, bias, fear, misinformation, laziness, spin, celebrity worship, media overload, indebtedness, the cult of consumerism, a runaway ego - all add layers of grime, blocking the view, limiting awareness to opportunities.

There are lots of examples of how a dirty lens can cloud judgment, making it almost impossible to make good decisions: not taking school, career, or relationship risks because of fear; missing investment opportunities due to lack of understanding; being afraid of trying something new because of past experiences; missing all sorts of fun, interesting activities because they don't fit neatly into current routines.

Is a problem still a problem if you don't see it as a problem? When you allow your mind to dwell on the challenges, there will always be things to worry about and plenty of reasons not do something. The thinker has some control of the thought. Polishing the lens of perception demands a shift in the B.OS to focus on win-list items. Instead of scanning for what's missing in striving mode, try focusing on what's in place, working, and right, then figure out how to make that even better.

100

One time, a young relative was trying to choose a college to attend and I had hoped to encourage her. Having been to three colleges myself and received three degrees, I felt I had some insight to contribute and wanted to help out. I bought her a book on getting into college, hoping that would start a conversation. As months went by I heard tales of campus visits, but I was never brought into the discussion. I started to feel hurt and left out. My lens was dirty.

I have come to understand that they were not excluding me so much as making a decision to keep their discussions within their immediate family. By taking it personally, I had created stress for myself and projected an expectation on them that pushed us apart. It was hard to let go but let go I did. With a clean lens, I feel grateful for my friends and family as they are, not as I wish they would be.

Getting past bias, fear, ego, and all the raindrops of pain, guilt, sadness, stress, and anxiety is about seeing and accepting the stories from our past, and present, then realizing they do not dictate the future. Limits are almost always self-imposed. Cloudy thoughts will always be coming and going. Get used to simply noticing them, look for the silver lining, but don't deny the messages they bring. Deal with them and remember there is always blue sky just beyond the gray.

Some policies are easy and stick naturally. Others will come under attack from policy parasites working against your best efforts to make changes. These barrages are waged by negative people or your not-so-friendly neighborhood inner-critic. All fed by fear, uncertainty, and doubt.

People who resist your attempts to evolve are a very real obstacle to your transformation. You have to consciously fight back. Realize that challenging people will get in the way. Avoid negative people, beliefs, behaviors, and outdated anchors like the plague. Say no to negativity.

Part of having a clean lens is being able to see (and avoid) the people that don't work for you. Whatever the situation, challenge, or people involved, a clean lens brings awareness to the reality of personal priorities. You realize you can't have it all, but there is plenty to go around.

Wisewords: *"Truth is like the sun. You can shut it out for a time, but it's not going to go away."* ~Elvis Presley

≈ Trust Natural Intuition

Have you ever looked back on a decision and said, "*I knew that was a bad idea?*" How many times have you been in a job, relationship, or living situation that you knew was not supporting your best self? Well, if you're like me, this has happened a lot.

No matter how hard you try, there is no way to know all the facts about anything. At some point, you need to let go of knowing and let intuition drive. This is the ability to sense or know something without direct experience or intellectual reasoning. Intuitive intelligence is a form of pattern recognition based on experience and awareness. It is an insight or understanding beyond experience and knowledge, a bucket into the well of wisdom. Intuitive intelligence can be part of your everyday win-list visioning and a powerful partner.

Try it for yourself sometime. Go for a bike ride or a drive with no destination in mind. Head to the thrift store or call a friend with no agenda. Take a trip with just a little planning and lots of unscheduled days. Surrender decision-making and let intuition guide where you turn, stop, shop, talk, and then see where you show up. Nine out of ten times, you will find yourself just where you need to be before you even knew you needed to be there!

~~~

After college and a stint working in a Tahoe casino, I decided to move to the Bay Area near family. It seemed like a good plan as the technology revolution was gearing up in nearby Silicon Valley. Rolling down Highway 80 just into Sacramento, the old Buick started smoking and screaming as a wheel bearing went out. The garage said it would take two days to get parts so I got a room and turned on the TV.

Hunger set in. A venture down Fulton Boulevard set me to thinking, "*This is a cool town. It seems big enough to have some opportunities and it would be a fresh start.*" I stayed twenty years. Found good work, great friends, and had many adventures in Sacramento. I went with it, followed intuition, and made some wonderful memories.

Was the bad wheel bearing a signal from the universe or maybe just a random accident? There was no way I would have stopped and stayed without that nudge. I'll never know what fortune would have found me in the late 1980's Silicon Valley, and I'm OK not knowing - all part of the magnificent mystery.

Any time is a good time to stop and check in with your intuitive guide. Ask, what is my next best move? When should I make that move? Your inner-fan will always steer you in the right direction. Any time there are feelings of fear, anxiety, greed, anger, or pain is a good time to specifically ask your inner voice for clear guidance. The answers may seem scary or difficult. Trust. When things settle out, it will all make sense.

Intuition is an instinct. Like Jack Sparrow's compass in the "Pirates of the Caribbean" movies, it always points to the treasure: health, connection, wealth, happiness, success, peace-of-mind. You have this compass in your pocket right now; ask and it will show you the way.

Wisewords: *"Your time is limited, so don't waste it living someone else's life. Don't be trapped by dogma - which is living with the results of other people's thinking. Don't let the noise of other opinions drown out your own inner voice. And most important, have the courage to follow your heart and intuition."* ~Steve Jobs

≈ Tapping Inner Wisdom

One of the most demanding parts of life is having to make decisions on matters in which the consequences may be quite large. But, there are multiple relevant factors, huge unknowns, and no foolproof method for making choices. This requires wisdom.

Wisdom is simply seeing the world as it is. As simple as this sounds, it is nearly impossible to see everything clearly. Our lens of perception is always clouded by stories, beliefs and preconceived notions that distort reality. Being wise sounds like a lofty skill reserved for professors or philosophers, but it's really more of a practical goal to work towards as a strategy for enjoying life.

Studying happy older people paints a connect-the-dots picture to learn about wisdom. Some poor decisions have taught them how to make good ones. They have discovered you can't be, see, do, and have everything. The awareness of experience has taught them to make selective choices about how and with whom to spend their precious time. They've learned to do more of what sparks curiosity, feeds the soul, and brings joy while doing less of what brings them down, creating stress or sorrow.

Wisdom is the ability to recognize truth without proof. It is a capacity to apply information, knowledge, experience, discretion, empathy, and intuitive intelligence all at once. Wise people take what they feel and know then transform it into the essence of who they are. They are patient knowing it sometimes feels like things will never change, but then they always do.

~~~

Wisdom often boils down to judgment. Good judgment is the result of experience. Experience is often the result of bad judgment, so there is no such thing as failure, only stepping stones to wisdom. Eleven characteristics of wise people include:

1. Realistic about how unique people are and how hard life can be.
2. Hold a positive attitude and expectations about life and aging.
3. Ability to see the core of issues but don't try and convert or influence others.
4. Self-acceptance, a knowingness of nature, quirks, what works, and what doesn't.
5. Sincere, direct, and generous with understanding the pressures on others.

6. Look for commonalities instead of differences.

7. Actions are consistent with his/her values and ethical beliefs.

8. Not complainers. Accept situations, people & luck (good/bad) without judgment.

9. Appreciate all things. Able to be grateful and savor even the little things.

10. Realistic about what can be accomplished & able to focus on what's necessary.

11. Steady. Calm. Resilient. Quick to laugh at themselves. Slow to anger or panic.

What does it mean to be wise? The simple answer is to be honest and without bias. To be able to honestly see and reflect on strengths, weaknesses, and the needs of all is an art. You have to be willing to step back, accept responsibility, observe the blind spots, question beliefs, and strip back layers of ego expectations.

Blind spots are things we miss, though often obvious to others. These mental dark corners are shaded in the rationalizations used for comfort. They are areas where we feel inadequate or uncomfortable exploring. They are what we resist confronting, but needs to be seen and worked through.

Success in any area typically breeds entitlement blind spots. These ego glitches unconsciously shift a moral compass off course. Entitlement blinds one's ability to see the needs of all concerned. Wise people stay mindful of this mindless aspect of human nature. They know they have blind spots, prejudices, and biases, then do the work needed to hold on to values and see things clearly. Wise people don't feel victimized but rather live in acceptance and appreciation.

Wisdom always comes back to love. Wise thinking knows at its core that the answer to every question is love. Whether looking inward at the self or outward at others, no matter what is at stake wisdom circles back to love. Sometimes it takes tough-love to make progress. Letting love cradle fear builds strength, comforts and carries one through hardship. Love follows the golden rule guided by compassion, kindness and non-attachment. When in doubt about what to say or think simply ask, what would love do?

As life winds down, love is the force that holds our hand when facing yet another transition. A lot of the fear of passing comes from worrying about losing all the people and things built up over a lifetime. As wise people get older, they consciously love, forgive and let go of attachments. Forgiveness calms the mind, releases anger

105

and fear. Seeing friends and family pass takes some of the mystery away. The possibility of spirit living on is comforting. Knowing the ultimate punch line will come brings reality home, firing the desire to live fully now.

Wise elders have learned how to keep actions and attitude in alignment with reality, to stop doing the things that don't serve them, and do more of the things that do. Experience has taught many seniors to enjoy life simply because they do not have a lot of time left. Wherever you are at in life, asking for wisdom delivers a map and a plan. It opens doors and delivers peace.

Can one will themselves to be wise? Hard to say, but act wise and odds are that you will get similar results.

Wisewords: *"There is nothing the wise man does reluctantly."* ~Seneca

≈ Strategic Retreat

Sometimes after making investments in time, money, and resources, it becomes clear that hopes or plans are just not working out. When do you let go?

The classic glass of water analogy offers a smart perspective on stress and anxiety. It goes like this: it's easy to pick up, sip, and hold a glass (of worry, guilt, frustration) for a little while. The longer you hold on, the heavier it feels. Try to hold it for an hour or a day. It becomes hard, then impossible. Stress and worry are the same - the longer you hold on, the heavier the heart gets.

What would it feel like to give yourself permission to set some glasses down, if even for only a minute? Issues with siblings, parents, work, or spouse - set them down. Worries about finances, adult children, or lovability - set down that heavy load. Be present. Only after setting them down can you feel how heavy they have been. The issues will be there to pick up again. Take a break.

Check in to see how great it feels to be free of desire to control or change things that may not be changeable. Find lightness in simply folding laundry, making a meal, enjoying the drive without worry or stress in the background.

Maybe we can get a lesson from our animal friends. They live, play, enjoy, suffer, and die but do not seem to get stressed out or worry about much. Their lives aren't complicated; they eat when they are hungry and sleep when tired. Instinct rather than anxiety govern their few preparations for the future.

As far as we can tell, animals are just busy doing what they do in the moment, not worried about life's meaning, the past, or the future. They have a simple survival policy and stay focused on that. For the animals' happiness lives in the now, not in the promise of some future joy lying ahead.

Stress is the enemy. It clouds the lens of perception while fostering bad decisions. Left unchecked, worry and anxiety grind away silently in the background leading to burnout. The wisdom is in learning how to set the glass down.

It's easy to get locked into a path once a decision is made. New information demands being open to changing directions. Maybe your ego is tied up in it or afraid what others will think. Allow yourself to let it go. This is your life. Sometimes one step back is smarter than two steps sideways. Strategic retreat is a healthy way to drop the stress, regroup, refocus, and rock on.

I once had a thriving business in an industry I enjoyed. There were challenges but overall the work paid off with a flexible schedule and steady income. At the time, a long-term romantic relationship was ending and I was feeling confused. In the middle of the break up, an offer came in to buy the business. It was a hard decision, but selling seemed to be a good move, a fresh start. Then the recession hit.

A lot of the money I had made vanished in the stock market. I felt totally lost. My fiancé and business were gone. Without them, who was I? I could not find a job and all the thinking in the world could not solve the dilemma. I decided to move south to reconnect with family. Strategic retreat.

This decision took a lot of work to make happen. Sell everything, rent out the house, say goodbye to good friends. Ego had a few things to say about a man in his 40's moving home. The voices of regret and the inner-critic spoke to me non-stop, nearly driving me crazy.

Being around family brought its own challenges, but turned out to be a good decision. A stable, loving environment created the space and desire to get on with life, write this book, and whatever is to follow that.

I later realized that subconsciously I was creating discomfort to force some changes that needed to happen. Retreat was the path forward. It took a few years of transition to come out on the other side. In many ways, it still feels like a story in progress, but instead of stress there is hope.

Sometime I wonder where my business would have been if I had stayed on that track, but that is a fool's curiosity. Psychologist Carl Jung defined happiness as living in harmony with who we are meant to be. This takes time and honest perspective, space that can be found in strategic retreat.

Learn how to put the glass down. Let worries flow away. The sooner you let go, the faster you'll be free. Every time you set a cup or glass down in our physical world, let that be a reminder to let go of some weight, sit up straight, shake off some stress and savor the present. On the other side of your pain is something good.

Wisewords: *"A setback is nothing but a setup for a comeback!"* ~Willie Jolley

≈ Just Breathe

Clarity arises from stillness in the same way that confusion arises from chaos. Peace and contentment exist within us at all times. It's just that so much noise is made looking for it that we drown out the silence. For more clarity, invite stillness in. One way to do this is through meditation.

Nearly everything in this book leads back to rigging the game to reframe expectations that serve true needs. None of this can happen in a freewheeling, stormy monkey mind. Our big brains naturally want to race and solve problems. Even when things are going good, our mind can feel chaotic. It often creates imaginary difficulty to stay busy.

The clarity we seek arises from stillness. To get your B.OS attitude right, the mind needs to unwind, be calm, rested, and recharged. This experience of a peaceful mind is not limited by circumstances in life, but rather by a willingness to learn how to pause and listen.

Pause to rest the mind and you will feel better. This is no great mystery, yet it is amazing how much time we spend looking after our physical health and how little attention we give to mental wellness. When thoughts are still, there is no room for wanting, wishing, regret, blame or anger. The mind has limitless potential to appreciate and enjoy life. Meditation simply helps us to remember and realize it.

Meditation gives you the opportunity to get to know yourself. It is an exercise in listening. It slows thinking down long enough for the mind to hear itself. It helps us understand how and why we behave the way we do, and how to behave better. It builds up the thalamus, that part of the brain that controls the cerebral cortex and regulates consciousness. It has been clinically shown in mindfulness based stress reduction (MBSR) programs to reduce inflammation, increase blood flow to support synaptic activity, and much more. Meditation polishes a silent, nourishing mirror for the mind.

~~~

A meditative mantra or silence is not the absence of thought, it's more about not actively engaging, resisting, or pursuing thoughts. I've found meditation is a magnifying glass showing everything in more detail - the good, the bad, the ugly, and the beautiful; all of it there to see and accept.

Introspection is not about acquiring anything; it is about letting go. It's not work but more an enjoyable, playful curiosity that's easy to stick with because it works and feels good. It's not about getting some result; it's more about intention and attitude. Get this approach right and everything else will take care of itself.

Meditation is not only for the difficult times, but also a tool to appreciate and reflect on success with a mindful release of attachment. It raises your state of bliss awareness - that giddy feeling of physical, emotional, mental and spiritual happiness from within.

Lots of prominent business people, celebrities, scientists, and sports champions have publicly spoken out about the benefits of meditating. People such as Richard Branson, Arthur Ashe, Anderson Cooper, George Lucas, Dr. Neil deGrasse Tyson, Clint Eastwood, Ellen DeGeneres, Kobe Bryant, Jerry Seinfeld, Oprah Winfrey, Sheryl Crow, and many others actively promote the creative awareness that comes with meditation. Just look at this list. These people are the leaders in their field. Many have said they were able to conquer fear and anxiety through self-awareness practice. Meditation works.

Think of it as tuning your instrument or plugging your battery into the Unified Field for a relaxing, reorganizing recharge. Meditation and sleep form the space where experiences are averaged, memories cataloged and accounts balanced.

Research has definitively shown how simple conscious breathing meditation delivers massive long-lasting cognitive and psychological benefits. It can improve sleep, cut depression, lower blood pressure, anxiety, and add oxygen to the bloodstream. Sign me up.

~~~

Often I hear, "*I can't calm my mind enough to meditate,*" or, "*I don't have time*" or, "*I don't know how to meditate.*" The truth of those stories is that you just may not have discovered a style that works for you. Forget about finding the perfect meditative state of mind. It's only about developing a comfortable approach for you.

One way to explore intentional meditation takes advantage of something we do all day every day - breathing. It is like placing a small dam in front of the thought

110

stream, making, even for a moment, a calm reflecting pond in the mind where thoughts have a chance to fall into place, settling into the layers of the true-you.

Start by sitting calmly, feeling your body, then breathe in (through the nose), hold for a second or two, then release the breathe out (through the mouth) then hold again for a pause. When thoughts come up, just let them go.

Help your mind relax and refocus thoughts by balancing the breaths with four-part breathing. Breathe in thinking, "*breathing in*" (pause & hold), then breathe out thinking, "*breathing out*" (pause & hold). Repeat.

Or, try counting each breath in and out up to ten, then start over at one. Meditation releases ego attachments. These are not you. Both techniques are examples of ways to push out ANTs, distract the monkey, slow thinking, and open the mind.

It is a good way to start the day and easy to do almost anywhere, even in urgent situations, delivering the ability to respond instead of react. It is also a foundation for more advanced mantra or intentional affirmation meditation.

It might be hard to quiet your mind between breaths at first. Don't worry about it. Just feel the release and accept whatever comes through. It is like trying to go to sleep - the harder you try, the less likely you are able to nod off. There is no good or bad, right or wrong way to meditate, there is only distracted and not distracted; you will be able to tell the difference.

When distractions arise and thoughts drift, simply let them go and re-center. Distraction is simply an opportunity to remember to stay present. With just a little practice, you'll be able to sit with confidence and drop into a meditative state quickly.

It's funny how just paying attention to breathing actually quiets the monkey long enough to chill. Even physical pain has been shown to be reduced with this technique. Breathe in acknowledging the pain, hold, then breathe out releasing the pain. That feeling when our body relaxes and the mind lets go is a beautiful thing. Whenever you're done meditating, try to pause, reflect, remember, and hold on to that centered feeling.

In other forms of meditation, the practice is a bit more structured. A common recommendation is to sit twice a day for about twenty minutes, set a timer, close your eyes, wait about half a minute, then start chanting a mantra, thinking it in your mind, or in some combination of the two, over and over again. At the end of meditation, stop thinking the mantra and wait about 2 minutes before opening your eyes. This hypnotic state is clinically shown to relax and energize the mind.

Meditation is a way to remember that everything is perfect just as it is. It releases the desire to change, fix, pursue, or destroy anything. It creates time to rest in the state of complete acceptance and gratitude without plans or purpose.

~~~

Writing about meditation got me thinking about other ways to practice and build mindfulness in everyday living. This seems to happen when an activity takes some focus, technique, challenge, or precision, but not a lot of problem-solving concentration. Just as counting breaths stops the thinking there are lots of activities that tune in the larger awareness connection. Walking meditation, crafting, coloring, instrumental music (listening and playing), art, dancing, and exercise all seem to be natural paths to relaxing the mind.

Mindless thoughts tend to be played by the inner-critic. Mindfulness practice coaxes the inner-fan out, encouraging a regular dialogue with your higher self. Meditation shows us how to be at ease with things as they are while staying open to the way they can be. Consciously upgrading your B.OS brings awareness to the surface where positive self-image can be defined, recognized, reinforced, and celebrated.

The sense of calm that insight meditation delivers becomes useful when we apply it to our sense of everyday awareness and relationships. It sews a mindful spaciousness that quiets inner drama. The more space you create in your mind, the more space you will find in living. The quiet mind is an open and fertile place where the present is savored and the path forward is obvious.

Wisewords: *"Prayer is when you talk to God. Meditation is when you're listening."* ~ Kelsey Grammer

≈ Mind Your Mantra

Just as our bodies need quality food and exercise to stay healthy, the mind needs to be taken care of as well. Using mantras, affirmations, maxims, proverbs, and wise sayings during meditation supercharges mental fitness.

They release the mind from thinking long enough to get clear, energized, and make connections. They clean the lens of perception to stay focused on filling in needs while finding patterns of being that work. Planting smart ideas forces out negativity and seeds the mind with intentions that support win-list thinking.

Mantras are Sanskrit/Hindu nonsense words or short phrases you are given or pick for yourself. The mantra may change as you become more self-aware. One often-used mantra is the tone, "*Om*." This syllable is an ancient Sanskrit sound that represents the sound of ultimate reality, truth, knowledge, and oneness with the universe and peace in the soul.

Affirmations are similar to a mantra but more specific and targeted to whatever you are going through or want to develop right now. They are positive, present tense statements that can change your brain structure on a cellular level.

Practicing affirmative antidote thoughts on a consistent basis helps focus attention on intentions, cement your policies, and insulate you from ANTs. What you tell yourself over time is what you believe.

Affirmations must be in alignment with your unique resources, nature, and situation, though. No matter how many redwood affirmations an acorn makes, it is still an oak.

~~~

One approach to focus the mind on intentional affirmations is Exchange Meditation ^{TM}. The exchange recognizes that what you give in this world is what you get.

Breathe in (< symbol for breathing in) feeling an affirmation, feel what you are willing to *give* (i.e., I am love, I trust, I forgive <). Then pause & hold the breathe for a second or two (/ symbol for the pause & hold), let the thought sink in and echo. Slowly breathe out (> symbol for releasing the breath), repeating the second half of the affirmation feeling what you *want* and plan to experience more of (i.e. > I am loved, I am trusted, I am forgiven). Then pause, set the glass down, hold the exhaled breath, letting the thought echo in silence. Repeat.

Or, try breathing in what you seek, hold, then breathe out what you want to release. Some examples include: "*Breathing in curiosity*"/ "*breathing out expectation.*" "*Breathing in humility*"/ "*breathing out arrogance.*" "*Breathing in compassion*"/ "*breathing out judgment.*" "*Breathing in gratitude*"/ "*breathing out entitlement.*" Pair the thoughts you want to upgrade with breathing until they echo in the subconscious, guiding beliefs, setting expectations, and driving real-time living.

The pause in four-part breathing is where magic happens. The space between breaths is like the space between notes in music. Only because of the breaks in a tune can you hear the melody. This echo space reveals the quiet hidden beneath mental chatter. Without space, thoughts become noise. The pause ends as the next note appears, changing the one just passed, giving it meaning, marching on. Cause, effect, cause, effect...

One of my favorite affirmations delivers daily guidance by helping see the world in the best light while reminding me to embrace life with a curious playfulness in my heart: "*I see through eyes of bright </> My heart is warm and light.*" In this case, to "*see through eyes of bright*" means to look for, pay attention to, invest in, and try to copy examples of the brighter side of human nature: acceptance, selflessness, responsibility, gracefulness, empathy, love, nurturing, optimism, creativity, etc. "*My heart is warm and light,*" reminds us to check ego at the door, to be a grateful and positive force in any situation, while maintaining a light heart, free of fear or regrets.

You are what you believe. Beliefs set the boundaries. Affirmations work consciously on a subconscious level to rewire beliefs and expand the range of possibilities. Pick two or three affirmations that apply to your current situation or state of mind and repeat them while four-part breathing for a few minutes before going to sleep at night and again first thing in the morning, even while still in bed. Mute the TV and do a round during commercials, while waiting in line at the market, during yoga. Any time is the right time to tune in.

If affirmations don't feel right, try holding a mantra or just one thought between the breaths. Thoughts like serenity, compassion, joy, curiosity, creativity, love, peace, or whatever resonates with your needs, will quiet the mind chatter while building wisdom.

As awareness grows, you will begin to spot more opportunities to stop and savor your personal park. You will find yourself acting consciously in real time instead of looking back and saying, "*I wish I had said/done/thought....*" For example, meditating on compassion will make you less judgmental and more tolerant of challenging people as stressful situations come up. Meditating on creativity or other abilities helps spot options and opportunities in time to grab them.

Add some structure to building mindful intention by assigning an idea to each day of the week. Make Mondays about gratitude, Wednesdays about wonder, Fridays about no fear, Sundays about serenity. To become more subconsciously conscious, start each morning with intentional meditation, then include the same ideas in that day's journal notes.

Or, try holding an image of a still lake or calm mountain meadow. Simply saying "*thank you*" with genuine emotional gratitude between breaths delivers a vitalizing release.

Try a recorded guided meditation or leave the world of language altogether and simply hold a feeling of calmness, gratitude, and openness while meditating. It's perfectly fine to mix and match techniques for mindfulness à la carte. When you find yourself being pulled deeper, let go and be with it. After a while, every waking breath is an opportunity to release, relax, file, and refocus.

Try distilling your win-list down to its short and sweet essence during intentional breathing. Pay attention to what feels right and is working, then tweak your affirmation memes to capture personal knowledge and truth.

Research shows that simply reciting the prayer or mantra is not enough, though. Only when you regularly tune in with genuine belief and an emotional charge does the practice rewire the brain and open the mind. Most mindfulness experts recommend establishing a core practice routine and doing that regularly. Once established, gradually build on it as new approaches surface or needs change. Whichever meditation style, find ways to do it regularly and feel it at your core.

One example of the value of a regular practice routine is having a wake-up routine. Mornings have been a tough time of day for me off and on over the years.

For some reason I wake up thinking of lots of reasons why my life sucks. I think about what's missing, question decisions, feel I'm not good enough or simply not getting the breaks I feel I deserve. I'm not sure why this is, but I have heard of a similar experience from others.

Over the years I've figured out a system that really helps. Upon waking, instead of letting my mind wander aimlessly into the minefield, I start with a few minutes of simple four-part breathing. As consciousness invades, I'll throw down my morning prayer then a series of four exchange affirmations along with breathing, then run through a mental review of the current win-list. This quick routine gets me up and to the stove to start water for tea. As the water boils, then tea steeps, I'll sit and go a little deeper into whatever is coming up, or simply sit in breathing meditation. Once at my desk, I try to make a few notes in the journal, write a note to a friend or play a little music before digging into work. The days always get better, but this practice rigs the game to help it happen faster and with less stress..

No matter how well we live our life it can sometimes still feel unjust and unfair. Unfortunately, there's no one truly able to watch out for you but you. It boils down to what expectations you bring and how to respond to what actually happens.

Meditation helps reset self-centered feelings and go to gratitude. It is one powerful way to bring perspective to the past, paint the future, and deliver B.OS upgrades. It flexes the wisdom muscle. Look around, try different styles, or create your own.

Wisewords: *"It's amazing how much you can learn if your intentions are truly earnest."* ~Chuck Berry

> Activity: Affirmations for Transformation

We are always telling ourselves stories - it's human nature. The problem is these snippets are often unconsciously based on fears or limiting beliefs that don't serve true needs. Some of these memes might include:

I'm not good enough. I'm not ready. I don't want to.

I'm unlucky in _____ (love, work, etc.)

I don't feel accepted based on what I do/have/who I know.

These thoughts and others put off the self-acceptance that is critical for happiness.

This activity and practice is used to identify core affirmations and maxims that rewire beliefs to resonate with your needs. These open the kind mind to believing that you have enough and all is perfect as is. These must be:

1. In the present tense (as though it is already that way).

2. Emotionally charged with conviction. (more feeling than thinking)

3. Part one (giving) <breathe in/hold/breathe out> Part two (receiving).

* If "*I am...*" statements don't feel right, try "*may I...*" to ask for guidance.

Pillar: Health - A tool to use when seeking to promote healthful living.

Affirmation examples: (giving) I relax. </> (receiving) I am at peace.

I treat my body right. </> My heart is strong and light.

I am patient. </> I am at peace.

Affirmation: I _____

Pillar: Relationships - Love and trust your way to healthy connections.

Affirmation examples: I AM love. </> I AM loved.

I trust. </> I am trusted.

I forgive. </> I am forgiven.

I listen. </> I am heard.

Affirmation: I _____

Pillar: Resources - Attract an abundance of whatever you really need.

Affirmation examples: I serve. </> My resources serve me.

I am resourceful. </> I have what I need.

I am in the right place. </> It is the right time.

I forgive debts owed to me. </> I share in abundance.

Affirmation: I _____

Pillar: Responsibility - Make good choices happen naturally.

Affirmation examples: I AM the cause. </> I AM the cure.

I make my life meaningful. </> I feel grateful every day.

I am awake. </> I am in awe.

What I give. </> Is what I get.

Affirmation: I _____

Pillar: Creativity - Release your creative fun self.

Affirmation examples: I am in the flow. </> I am in the know.

I am awake. </> I am open.

I set my intentions. </> I reap the benefits.

Affirmation: I _____

In addition to meditation, try writing affirmations on the bathroom mirror or on a sticky note in the kitchen, car, or office. Say them throughout the day to calm and channel the thought stream. I've also seen people set alerts on their phone, wear jewelry or place colorful stickers here and there as reminders to stop and refocus.

Short affirmation abbreviations can also be used as logins or passwords to keep the ideas front and center: Peace4Me!, 1am14love, Ok2relax.

The only thing we have any real control over are thoughts. Thoughts are things. Change starts one breath at a time, one thought at a time. Using breathing affirmations whenever you can grab a minute or two will help keep an even keel. It can also help to get the mind calm and focused right before an important activity or interaction.

Another ritual to help manage the mind is adding short prayer affirmations into your daily routine. This is one easy way to build a gratitude reflex. Reaffirming belief and trust that all is right makes it so. These tools help align energy and tune up attitude. Just as you have to stop to tune a guitar or sharpen the saw, building in these regular B.OS updates rigs the game to happily do what's necessary.

There are also three prayers that I use everyday. I sometimes use the word "*God*" in these, not because of a particular religious affiliation, but because it feels right for me, an easy shorthand for connection to the higher power I know exists. If saying "*God*" doesn't work, you can replace it with, "*Great Spirit, Creator, Holy One, My Higher Power, Universe, Angels,*" etc.

There is no better way to begin the day than quieting the mind and letting go of the past to start with a fresh perspective. One to say in the morning while still in bed: "*Thank you. Thank you. Thank you for this new day, its beauty and it's light. Thank you for a chance to begin again. Free me from the limitations of yesterday, for today I am reborn. I accept, am grateful, and give thanks for all that is.*" This, along with some breathing meditation, usually gets the head right before feet hit the floor.

Sometimes short and sweet is best. One for the morning, or any time really is: "*Thank you for filling my heart with compassion and loving kindness.*" The key here is asking for compassion and kindness to yourself. We are often hardest on ourselves and can't really show up for others without self-acceptance.

Before each meal try: "*Thank you for this food and how it helps bring mind, body, spirit, thoughts, words, and actions in alignment with dreams and highest purposes.*"

And then at night, before drifting off consider trying something like: "*Thank you for this day now over, may all the love remain. Thank you for health, happiness, gratitude, deep peace, and the opportunity to serve again tomorrow.*"

These rituals help bring form to the formless, making the ideas and feelings real. Try adding current win-list details to help keep the inner-fan sharp, accepting, and grateful in the reality zone.

Wisewords: *"Our life is what our thoughts make it."* ~Marcus Aurelius

≈ Get Lucky

Making excellent life decisions in alignment with the true-you is the foundry where luck is forged. Too often, we wait for luck to find us, hoping it will lead to good stuff happening. As it turns out, luck isn't something that happens to a few fortunate ones, it's the visible symptom that shows up in people who rig the game to live in their park.

Good luck is as real as bad luck. Maybe you were in the right place at the right time, maybe you weren't. Maybe you had some help or made some great decisions, maybe you didn't. Wishing things were different will not make them so. Life is not predestined, or random, there is some element of both. You have many possible futures. Luck lives where preparation meets opportunity. As far as this book goes, this involves getting real with yourself, understanding needs, and building policies across all five pillars.

Luck is the fork in the road, the inkling, the spark before the flame. It springs from the routine of a life being lived fully. Try these six steps to spot and leverage luck:

1. See opportunity everywhere. Open up your mind to "*see*" and "*feel*" connections beyond the obvious. Don't classify, judge or pre-suppose situations or people. Stay awake and aware to find lucky (unexpected) paths.

2. Prime the pump. Read magazines, talk with strangers, get lost, explore ideas, stay positively open to the unknown, then take action when opportunity knocks.

3. Say yes! Most of our internal dialogue is a competition between intrigue (yes) and anxiety (no), curiosity (yes) vs. caution (no). Luck chases yes.

4. Release attachment. Luck may show up dressed for a party as you leave for school. Don't expect it to fit neatly into plans in an obvious way. Luck rarely drops into your lap with a big red bow. Be ready to pull on a thread, to follow a hunch and see where it leads.

5. Take a break. Open space is the land where luck dwells. Relax. Break routines. There is a time to be a conscientious worker, student, husband, wife. And, there is the freewheeling time without obligations, plans or agendas - lucky time.

6. Figure out how to clean your lens of perception to see the silver lining. A good attitude is the horse that pulls your lucky cart. Waiting for lucky things to find you is the path to disappointment. Lead by unique example and the right people will join in, bringing along lucky situations.

Spend time exploring the ideas, people, projects, and activities that spark interest. Look for opportunities to be curious about filling current needs. Pay attention to which threads feel right, then pull on them. When things don't work, let them go. When new opportunities present themselves, be discerning yet prepared to jump on them. By fully showing up as your lucky, authentic self, there's no difference between what you are capable of being and what is actually being. That is bliss.

Wisewords: *"I'm a great believer in luck, and I find the harder I work, the more I have of it."* ~Thomas Jefferson

5. Be Here Now

William Shakespeare said, *"Tis nothing good or bad but thinking makes it so."* It seems the bard was onto something here. Happiness is one of those funny things - the more you chase after it, the trickier it becomes to find. Those of us trained to pursue pleasure often end up on the hamster wheel running, but never quite able to get there. We get a taste and want more, but can't figure out how to run fast enough to keep the happy feelings coming. There is no fast enough.

So much has been written about the pursuit of happiness - more than 4,000 books a year on average. With so much research, it should be easy for everybody to put the happiness pieces in place and sail smiling into the sunset. A quick look around reveals a mixed picture of happy, sad, bored, complacent, and anxious people. Modern society itself has created an environment fostering much unhappiness, and that feeling seems to be spreading around the world due to globalization.

The pharmaceutical companies want us to believe that chemical imbalances are the problem behind our moods and that pills are the answer. This is true for some, but not for most.

One approach is to forget the pursuit of happiness altogether. Research shows that people who chase happiness through distraction, money, drugs, sex, consumerism, etc. are focused too much on themselves. Striving for it damages relationships and makes you feel lonely.

When expectations match reality, happiness happens. Stop wanting anything from anybody. Release others to be themselves and focus on being the best possible version of yourself. The sooner you get comfortable feeling all of life, fueling true needs while paying attention to the needs of others, the sooner happy feelings will find you.

For more life satisfaction, be satisfied with what you already have. Appreciate where you are and what you have now. Give thanks for what is working and focus on activities that bring you joy and peace of mind. Look for the people and organizations that need your help, then give that help freely.

Find a path or spiritual practice that opens your heart to the larger connection, then practice it. Refocus the lens to feel happiness without the need for approval or the desire to acquire more people, stuff, or experiences. This will feel like a breakdown to some. But breakdowns lead to breakthroughs.

However you find it, well-being not only feels good but is good for you - lowering stress, inflammation, and blood pressure. Healthy minds have learned to accept and be amused by challenges and blessings alike. They stay curious and push themselves into the glorious unknown with positive expectations.

In these chapters, we'll see how ego and emotions are signals, not conditions. Explore the free power available from fear and gratitude. See how becoming a change agent can satisfy needs while making your world a better place.

Wisewords: *"I went to a bookstore and asked the saleswoman, 'Where's the self-help section?' She said if she told me, it would defeat the purpose."* ~George Carlin

≈ Emotions as Signals

Emotions are often perceived as mere feelings when they are actually doorways to self-awareness. Identity is often based on emotional state. Mental turmoil is painful, distracting, and zaps energy reserves. Emotionally satisfied people tend to look rested, have a strong identity, ambitions, and will generally admit to being happy most of the time.

Think of yourself as a mechanic who listens to the hum of a car's engine for clues to what needs fixing. In this case, you are the mechanic and the car, sensing and adjusting on the fly. Stressful emotions signal that something is either broken or needs to be tuned up. The feeling may pass but will always reappear until the underlying need is satisfied. Exploring and resolving emotions keeps your motor running smoothly.

A big part of minding your mood involves getting expectations in order. There is a measure of the difference between desired reality and true reality known as a schism. Schism, derived from the Greek "*schízein*" means to split. This cognitive dissonance is a measure of how much our thoughts are at odds with feelings, the division between you and yourself. "*You*" being your fantasy-idealized thoughts of what you want to do, have going on and wish to be. "*Yourself*" being who you are at present, and what the future realistically holds.

A schism of 10 describes a total separation between you and yourself, someone who is crazy or psychotic. A schism of 0 is one who lives and appears authentically in the world as they truly are. The higher the number, the more stress you will have in your life; the lower the number, the more peace you will have. One of the goals of policy setting is to help push your schism closer to zero.

~~~

There are eleven emotional trigger feelings that signal a schism in the red zone: anxiety, depression, regret, fear, anger, frustration, guilt, inadequacy, hate, loneliness and boredom. These are feelings, not facts. They are not attacks or conditions you are stuck with. Don't take them personally. These biochemical signals are looking out for your well-being, reminding intuition about unmet needs. We can let disappointments rule the day or reframe expectations and make them go away.

These cannot be ignored. If you are always trying to get away from difficult feelings or emotions, how will you ever fully understand and deal with them? For example, boredom is a signal that what you have been doing no longer serves you, that you will benefit by seeking out deeper experiences or new passions. Or that it may simply be time to relax without feeling the need to be productive. Trigger emotions are opportunities to figure out what is wrong, missing, or could be better. Imagine a world where you are able to witness thoughts and feelings without feeling controlled or overwhelmed by them.

On the flip side are the ten emotions that signal you are doing things right: happiness, joy, optimism, enthusiasm, curiosity, gratitude, amusement, pride, sympathy, and love. These feelings are like gravity pulling toward your happy place and pulling it toward you. When you feel these signals, make note on your win-list. These are the scripts used to train the inner-fan.

Buddha talked about emotional suffering as Dukkha, represented by the friction of a potter's wheel that regularly falls out of balance and rubs, unable to spin freely. Everybody's thoughts are a little bit out of balance most of the time. The skill is in learning not to dwell on emotions or be regretful, but rather to notice the feelings as a signal to find, fix and re-balance.

Emotional trigger feelings make us feel isolated, alone in the fight. Small adjustments make a big difference, but entropy will always warp the spin. Wisdom is accepting the unbalanced madness and being at ease with imperfection. If only we could see the madness in the minds of others, we would probably feel much more relaxed about our own crazy thoughts.

~~~

Sometimes, as much as we want, things don't go the way we want. As the saying goes, shit happens. Looking back, it's obvious my insecurities were the result of trying to get life to conform to some mythical version of how I thought it should be. It's easy to look back and see what could have been done differently. Until they invent a time machine, this knowingness can only serve to guide better decisions here and now in the land where regrets are wrangled.

Joy, sadness, anger, fear, disgust, and surprise are emotions hard-wired in from birth. Guilt, shame, contempt, and regret are not natural in the mind. Babies do not feel ashamed, guilty, or regretful. These learned feelings are based on where you were raised, who raised you, and all your life experiences. They feel real as we try to fit in and conform to social norms, but don't have to rule attitude. Self-loathing can be un-learned. Pursuing wisdom offers a plan to change perceptions. To help zero in on what to focus on, let's look at the big regrets that plague many people, especially as they age:

1. Not chasing dreams.

2. Not allowing themselves to feel and express feelings to others.

3. Working too hard and too long in life. Not making time to live.

4. Not staying in touch and continuing to invest in friendships.

5. Not taking care of their mind, body, and finances.

6. Forgetting that happiness is a choice.

Though these problems seems obvious, I've found myself struggling with all of them. Being true to yourself, taking time to smell the roses, reaching out, and expressing feelings just doesn't come naturally for everyone. This list gets me thinking about what regrets do I really want to avoid? What will be important for peace of mind in the twilight years?

The thing to remember is that older people regret the opportunities they didn't take far more than the risks they did try. I've come to realize that these needs can't be put off; there just won't be enough time to make changes in the future. Awareness of the regrets you want to avoid fires up the motivation to take action now.

Consider Elizabeth Kübler-Ross's DABDA model of emotional stages to help tame regrets and put speed bumps into perspective. The cycle starts when a disappointment or something you perceive as "*bad*" happens, triggering emotions leading to the D in denial (includes avoidance, shock, fear). Over time, this shifts into the A in anger, the "*Why me?*" or "*How could they?*" statements. Next comes B in bargaining, where we start to put things into perspective, realizing the longer we wait the harder it will be. Then the second D, depression or delusion: feeling sad or thinking that maybe by ignoring something it will go away. As we realize that the problem has not gone away, the A stage of acceptance balances emotions in the reality zone and we get on with living.

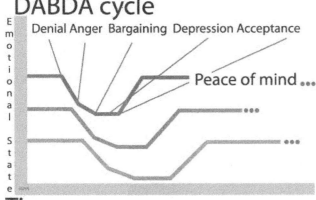

DABDA cycle

Understanding this cycle keeps feelings present to move us forward toward acceptance. Maybe the situation was beyond control to begin with. It does not matter. Ignoring pain does not make it go away. We simply have to go through the stages. If we don't, there will be regrets.

The actionable wisdom available here is that getting through the DABDA cycle does not have to take a long time. Moving through the stages can take a minute, an hour, a day, a week, years. Some people never get over disappointments. Feeling the anger and depression is essential to moving past it.

How long you let emotions rule your attitude is a policy you have some control over. This idea reminds me of an old Zen proverb: "*You can't stop the birds of sorrow from flying over your head, but you can stop them from making a nest in your hair.*"

Emotions are all about how you respond to what is going on. We always have the choice - be stuck or keep moving, feel sorry or choose to simply feel, acknowledge, retune, repair, release, and carry on.

Eighty five percent of the things we worry about never happen. DABDA awareness helps release the trivial stuff and speed up the resilience processor to deal with painful situations when they inevitably do happen.

Wisewords: *"Intellect may be confused, but emotions will never lie."* ~Roger Ebert

≈ Develop Healthy Ego Filters

Ego is simply an ever-changing thought system built on beliefs, experiences and expectations. It is a construct of the mind that can be negative, judgmental, or a supportive ally when embraced with awareness. It is one of the louder monkeys in the mind, usually responsible for bringing the opposite of whatever the higher self wants. It's often a sly trickster masquerading as an ally, telling you that the good life should come easily, even when you know there is work to do. Ego pushes; personal truth pulls.

Ego rebels when it perceives it's been deceived or taken advantage of. Ego-driven emotions can be a source of growth or an anchor tied to tired old programming. It decides whether or not to listen to intuition and how open the mind is to upgrades. It is the number one factor defining how clean or dirty the lens of perception is.

Ego filters claim ownership of the mind then keep us isolated for fear our secrets will get out, when in fact we all have the same secrets. These hallucinations trick us into thinking we know what is right for all concerned, placing expectations on ourselves, then imposing those expectations on others. In some twisted sort of way, this makes us feel in control, if even for just a minute.

Ego presents itself as the guardian when it's really the warden. An unchecked mindless ego invites the stinkin' thinkin' inner-critic to speak. The problem with self-focus is that just below the surface, your sub consciousness uses self-judgment to rate success. These judgments fire up doubt and fear, which short-circuits any chance of real transformation. Ego is not all bad or all of you, it just is.

At every moment there are two doors we can choose to walk toward in our thoughts, words, and actions: ego or spirit. The ego voices of extrinsic materialism trick our narcissistic future-based self into walking the endless chase towards a door we never quite get to and can never go through. There are also the voices of spirit, service, and independence vying for attention that lead us straight through the door to our higher selves.

It's funny how we try to think our way out of an overactive mind or make plans to be present at some future date. Awareness stops the cycle. Step back and see what's really going on. Life goes by quickly. You can spin wheels lost in ego thoughts or choose to be present and keep moving. Once you realize that ego is just another of the many voices we dance with, it gets easier to recognize ego motivations, play with them, and put then in their place by choosing to follow your heart. Ego can be tamed.

~~~

Ego is that part of Freud's primitive id, which is the aspect of personality that has been modified by the direct influence of the external world. It's a bridge between consciousness and unconsciousness. Ego is the most complicated human function and completely responsible for our sense of self-esteem and lovability. It defines who we are, the authorities we respond to, and what we are capable of.

The unobserved critic ego lives in the fantasyland of a self-centered you. It tends to think you can own or possess consciousness when it's more something to participate in and contribute to. It uses words like *'always'* and *'never'* which rarely are true. It throws joy out the window five seconds after you have experienced it and will seek thrills on the path of least resistance. It keeps us stuck in comfortable, old patterns. Stepping outside of ego thought traffic clears a space to relax, connect, and stop pushing so hard.

There are lots of aspects and dimensions to ego. The darker sides to watch for and learn to manage include: loneliness, denial, selective perception, belief substitution, monkey mind, grass is greener, loss aversion, judgment, and boxing-in. Nearly everyone struggles to overcome one or more of these patterns at one time or another.

When you slow down long enough to reflect on all the wonderful people and pieces of your life, not just what is happening this second, the insistent ego will quiet down. Focus on averaging experiences and win-list thinking instead of what's missing to make twice the progress in half the time. When the mind is quiet and grateful, it can see your present self as part of the larger whole, not just a single soul isolated in the current situation.

Learning to observe the ego mind at work requires courage, honesty, and openness without judgment, criticism or self-censorship. Modeling a positive, present, and aware ego is like learning to walk - every day gets easier.

I am reminded that though I may feel lonely at times, I am never alone on the path to self-discovery. Writing is a solitary act. I chose it without really knowing what I was doing or how much time it would take. Ego has tried to quit several times, but I'm not a quitter. When finished, I'll have a new work policy knowing that I need to look for a more social environment better suited to my nature.

Personally, I've come to believe that I'm never really alone. Maybe this is a coping mechanism, but so much quiet time has triggered a genuine feeling of connectedness beyond presence. All the people from my past and present are with me here now as we all march together into the future. Our paths will cross again and I will not be sitting here at the computer forever. Seasons will change and so will I, that knowledge is comforting. If ego feels alone or disconnected, maybe there is a reason. Try relaxing into the aloneness - go with it and see where it takes you.

~~~

There was once an Abraham Hicks workshop where a woman spoke about her aloneness. "*I don't get it. The more I want and need a relationship, the more I don't get one, and as soon as I no longer need one, it shows up.*" This is a wonderful example of how ego runs the law of attraction. As Mr. Hicks explains, "*When you are whole, in alignment and absolutely, perfectly happy standing on your own without needing a relationship, then they will come flocking to you. Because everyone wants to be with someone like that.*"

~~~

Inner-critic driven ego filters are built on illusions, fear, and delusions. Fear-based egos like to play the victim, complain, and keep you separate from others and from opportunities. They are arrogant, false, and boring; no fun at all.

Some of the brighter aspects of inner-fan based ego include: connectedness, selflessness, responsibility, gracefulness, empathy, love, nurture, optimism, and creativity. These patterns tap the free energy of the Unified Field to serve all who get good at living them.

Even a generally healthy ego gets defensive and snaps back when the world does not conform to what it thinks you deserve. It resists change and glorifies the past. It is responsible for all sorts of nutty behaviors that don't serve our higher purposes. It will defend bad choices at all costs. Negative ego voices are not you; they are learned patterns that can be changed with awareness.

By dissecting ego, you can see what stories cause you to react rather than respond. Start by asking ego to reveal itself and then pay attention. You will soon be able to feel the reaction impulse forming. Triggers being pulled and buttons being pushed will become signals to stop, release control, relax expectations, and choose to respond intentionally.

As awareness grows, it becomes easier to say to yourself, "*Well that's an annoying thought, accepted, but I'm not going to react and get caught up in it. Time to move on....*" Cultivating awareness delivers the power to skip past fears and old stories to eventually file them away from working memory.

It's critical to catch ego reactions early. Once it snaps and takes control of a situation, it's hard to back out. You say and do things that are not in alignment with the true-you, then set about defending thoughts that may or may not be based in reality. When you feel the bratty, small ego coming on, say nothing. Don't react. Don't respond. Pause, reflect, dismiss the inner-critic and invite your inner-fan to speak.

Did you know that when an airplane is on autopilot, it is off-course ninety percent of the time? It's true. The plane's computer is constantly correcting, bringing it back on course. It's the same with everyone - thoughts will drift. Belief drifts into doubt, plans slip into procrastination. The ability to pause, reflect, and refocus on smart policies will keep your flight plan true. This subtle art gets easier with practice and success. Awareness helps stay the course in real-time where it matters most.

~~~

I've come to realize that ego tends to think I deserve something (anything) better (different) than whatever I perceive is going on. This seems to be the root of a lot of fantasy vs. reality victim chatter, and the source of aimless striving. More self-awareness of ego's influence helps heal the split, bringing harmony to all the voices. Eventually, as you grow beyond the higher/lower self narrative, the mind can rest at one with all.

Have I mastered ego? Hell no. Awareness has delivered some control over it, but entitled thoughts are still there. When I become aware of a small ego mindset, no matter how "*good*" or "*bad*" the situation is, I'm still learning to pause and remember it is what it is, that all is well and right. There is no '*better life/situation/person*' over there. This is it; it's good and getting better.

It's not about trying to solve, fix, wait for or want anything to be different than it is. Allowing the ego to rattle on unobserved causes one to miss out on the joy here and now. It's like John Lennon said, "*Life is what happens when you're busy making other plans.*"

Maybe ego's evolutionary purpose is to keep us wanting more and pushing us forward. Without awareness, this drive can be a detour. The middle way is to have goals and dreams, but hold them lightly. Don't let aspirations interfere with the experience of the here and now. Observe ego to teach it how to savor simply, stay present, grateful, tolerant, and compassionate.

Consider the option of consciously nurturing a healthy ego based on inner workings, values, hopes, integrity, win-list, the true-you. These things cannot be threatened, lost, or taken away. It takes the same amount of energy to dwell on limits as it does to be grateful and visualize possibilities. The healthy ego draws from the past, keeping us present and on track toward the future you. It is a choice. Choose to tame the ego and be content.

Note: There is one interesting aspect of healthy ego that philosopher Friedrich Nietzsche called sublimation. This form of maturity is how socially unacceptable ego impulses, unrealistic idealizations, sexual, and status urges are converted to more meaningful thoughts, activities, and aspirations. Awareness is the answer. Using sublimation is one way to draw on the energy from base instincts to fuel higher social, artistic, and scientific accomplishment.

Wisewords: *"The true measure of a person is the degree to which they have managed to subjugate their ego."* ~Albert Einstein

≈ Practice Gratitude

Take a deep breath, hold it for two seconds, then, with feeling, exhale and release with an audible, "*thank you.*" How does that feel? Probably pretty good. The bond between gratitude and happiness is undeniable.

Research shows that people who practice a gratitude reflex have stronger feelings of control, self-acceptance, peace of mind, and purpose. It relaxes stress and depression while breeding healthful well-being. But just thinking grateful thoughts is not enough - you have to feel it.

Being awake and aware enough to savor, relish, and see everything through appreciation and gratitude clears and calms the mind. In other words, it's not so much about what you have to work with; it's about how you work with it.

You can make all sorts of wonderful plans for the future, but if you don't slow down to enjoy the present moments you will feel like you missed out - because you did. Awareness, acceptance, awe, and gratitude are industrial cleaners used to scrub the lens of perception to be grateful and present.

~~~

So what exactly is gratitude? How can one feel and express more? The dictionary definition says that because you appreciate what other people do for you, you are grateful. Gratitude is more complex than that. It comes from many sources, people, accomplishments, happy accidents, things that do and don't happen.

Things won't always go our way. Gratitude is the balance that helps maintain perspective. It is an inventory of what has worked and a divining rod pointing to what is important. It can be a decision-making filter that attracts good choices. It's common to invest in health, finances, and your career. Why not invest in gratitude as well?

Nurturing a grateful presence is fueled by an overwhelming sense of appreciation, awe, curiosity, and wonder. Research has shown how the feeling of reverence in the mystery of nature and all its creation cuts stress and expands our notion of available time. Recognizing beauty in the grand scheme squashes selfish little concerns.

Finding ways to savor joyful feelings, positive experiences, and fond memories helps capture win-list feelings that support the true-you. An attitude of gratitude can be much more than an occasional feeling, it can become a mindful state of being that helps organize reality into recognition of what's working and what's not. Learning to think through the gratitude filter helps rig the game by putting the past to work while bringing the future into focus.

Personally, I'm slowly learning to make acceptance, patience, compassion, and gratitude my all-day, everyday policies. All are must-have awareness's, not occasional feel-good things to do. Sometimes it's hard; life can be depressing. But when I'm quietly looking inward, I realize that I truly am grateful for the challenges and the rewards.

I'm finding that there are always ways to feel gratitude even in bad situations. For example, my mother's Alzheimer's has been tough to handle, but the gift has been more time with her and renewed relationships with some family members.

It is human nature to dwell on things. You can dwell on what's wrong or dwell on what feels right (win-list); it's a choice. Even though the mind is designed to solve problems, constant focus on what is missing or wrong will wear you down. Start seeing and believing you are the person you want to be, then let policies add detail to the design. This is not something you can wait until crisis hits then flip on. You need to dig the well before you are thirsty.

~~~

It is also human nature to focus on novelty, thus ignoring the normal. Everything we take for granted was once unusual and new. Often the hard work and effort it took to get you where you are is discounted. The great experiences are forgotten while expectation of what's next overwhelms subtle present joy.

Don't let a happy life become background scenery that is taken for granted. Pull out and polish the win-list daily. Savor, take credit, and give thanks as things do work out.

The ego mind is a funny thing; it quickly adapts to success and takes even the most splendid blessings for granted. Gratitude is the counterweight to ego. A simple awareness of how much quiet goodness is happening in the background puts ego's shiny object syndrome in its place.

When you do find yourself thinking about things that didn't work out as planned or hoped, look for ways to do it with gratitude and not regret. Learn. Release. Rock on.

I once had a medical procedure that required 24 hours of fasting before going in. The next morning, after being able to make my regular cup of tea, it struck me how much I enjoy and appreciate this little ritual. I decided then and there to make a policy to fast quarterly with the solstices and equinoxes. Not only does fasting deliver health benefits, but it has served to sharpen gratitude awareness of big and small things taken for granted.

The classic maxim, '*You don't know what you got until it's gone*' carries a lot of wisdom. Maybe you don't want to go as far as fasting, but try changing routines. One day try another tea, then see how much you enjoy going back to the one you love. Who knows, you might find a new tea to be grateful for. This process of breaking routines and trying new things builds up the spontaneous gratitude reflex response.

To build gratitude, be grateful. Drill down for deeper appreciations. If stuck searching for things to be grateful for, think up and down the gratitude chain. That tuna sandwich in your hand was brought to you by a trucker, a fisherman, and the ocean, all sources of easy gratitude. You may be grateful that the grocery store has so much wonderful food available. Open up to feeling grateful for the blueberries, the fresh milk, the farmer, the cow.

Be grateful for things that don't happen. That bus you missed might have had an accident. Hang pictures and enjoy mementoes as sources of inspiration, strength, perspective, and guidance. There is no limit and you cannot have too much. The more gratitude you allow to happen, the less space ANTs have to crawl around.

As great as gratitude is, it is not an instinct. It seems we are wired to focus on whatever is happening now and on what comes next, not to look back and give thanks.

We may be built to strive, but over time without pausing to savor, life loses its meaning. The idea is to consciously pause to generate as much gratitude and sublime sense of and awe as possible. As awareness grows there will be a crossover tipping point when it starts happening automatically, then builds on itself naturally. Worry fades away as it becomes obvious that most everything is perfect as is or will work itself out eventually. With the gratitude/awe reflex in place, it becomes easy to remember it is all good, and getting better. Gratitude is knowing that the grass under your feet is the greenest.

Some may call this feeling enlightened and it truly is a great place to be. Some will cross over and stay there, bravo. It's no surprise that for many this feeling comes and goes in direct relation to practicing the practice that gets you there. That's why rigging the game with policies like the EasyG Jar (see activity) work wonders.

Note: One of the many quirks of human nature is described by a funny word with a not so funny meaning. Schadenfreude (SHädən ˌfroidə), describes the unexpected thrill, feeling grateful (that it's not you), or deriving pleasure when witnessing or becoming aware of those less fortunate. The literal translation is: schaden, meaning to harm, and freude, meaning joyfully. This is a quirk of human nature in which our own perceived contentment has sometimes become dependent on others' situations. To compare is human. But question the source of that comparison: is it pity, jealousy, superiority, compassion, or love? Gratitude can be nurtured to higher levels in the heart. When tending your gratitude garden, watch out for this poison flower. Focus on tuning the heart to feel from the perspective of love.

Wisewords: *"I pray that you put your slippers way under the bed tonight, so when you wake up in the morning you have to get on your knees to reach them. And when you're down there, say thank you."* ~Denzel Washington

> Activity: EasyG Jar

Set up a clear vase or jar somewhere convenient where you will see it regularly. Every day scribble down something you are grateful for and throw it in. Every receipt, old post it, etc, can become a reminder to recognize and reflect on gratitude. What are the simple things to feel grateful for? Water, TV, coffee, electricity, chocolate, a song... make a note, throw it in the jar. A lover, child, friend, teacher, movie, sandwich... make a note, throw it in the jar. Every scrap of paper offers an opportunity to stop, wake up and give thanks for all the big and small things. Spot and note deeper appreciations for health, resources, relationships, creativity, or whatever comes to mind. The EasyG jar becomes a constant reminder of how great it is to live in gratitude. This activity rigs the game to notice and savor life, to see everything right. Tip the gratitude reflex by scanning for that which supports, not what is missing. Whenever feeling down or grumpy, note the jar and remember, "*I'm too blessed to be stressed.*" When my jar becomes full, I like to dump the scraps out, unfold and enjoy recalling the moments. Then burn I them and release the energy. Or try a gratitude bonfire by inviting friends to come relax, share, burn, release, and renew. Then start filling the jar all over again.

>Activity: Gratitude Garden Attitude Adjuster

Make a list of fond memories. Go back to your earliest memories of fun, friends, and family, reflecting on proud moments and what brought a smile. Think back to good times and happy accidents at the playground, at home, at camp, during summer trips, at work, wherever, whenever. Recall the people, places, and things that made an impression and trigger warm memories. These may have faded from consciousness, but are not forgotten. Use energy from the past to light up the present, average experience and shape the future. These themes and threads are the fabric of an evolving life. Draw on the memories any time. Use them to help shape a win-list. When in doubt, go to gratitude. Download the Gratitude Garden activity at PolicyPillars.com.

Wisewords: "*I cried because I had no shoes until I met a man who had no feet.*" ~Helen Keller

≈ Friend Fear

The universal law of attraction fails to care if you are having good, healthy thoughts or negative, fear-based limiting thoughts. The law says, "*like attracts like*," which sums up the idea that by focusing on positive or negative thoughts you get positive or negative experiences. Whatever thoughts we harbor and repeat become reality. Staying in a place of fear or doubt attracts exactly what you don't want!

How many times have you tried something scary and discovered that it was much easier than expected? Think for a minute about what you might be able to do without being afraid to try (make a new friend, start a business, explore a hobby, take a trip). Fear takes curiosity out of the race. When you trust the universe and accept everything as perfect in its imperfection, there is nothing much left to fear.

To put fear into perspective, realize that it is almost always based on imagination. The thing we often call fear is usually just some story or notion gone wild. Or some form of uncertainty. The unobserved ego loves certainty so when we don't know what is going to happen, ego will use fear to resist acceptance or exploration.

Accepting uncertainty opens doors to wonderful things. Smart fear knows when to be extra alert or avoid dangerous situations. It has also been shown to promote performance when embraced, as in a healthy competitive fear of failure. But that's it. Shift ego-based fear of uncertainty into a spirit of adventure and watch the outside world shift into a supporting role. Taking risks leads to rewards.

The word *'courage'* comes from the French word for heart. To be courageous is to have heart, to relax and be brave even when things are scary, unclear, or challenging. Try without knowing what will happen.

Friend F.E.A.R. to Feel Everything And Relax! Not addressing fears leads to the anxiety of knowingly avoiding potential. It's tough to conquer fear, but easy to be graceful in its wake. Taming and training the ego to embrace fear is one thing all wise people have in common.

Wisewords: "*Fear is static that prevents me from hearing myself.*" ~Samuel Butler

≈ Peace of Mind

While making the final edits on this book, I had to stop and ask, has this research and work stopped all the self-defeating voices in my head? I had to answer no. Some judgmental ego fear-based thoughts are still there. Writing has helped. But having ideas about what works is one thing, practicing is another.

Cultivating win-list thinking, creating meaning, managing expectations, and staying aware of the needs of others is always a work in progress. Mindless thoughts will happen less and less all the time. Sometimes I feel down or anxious about a current situation, but am getting much quicker at quieting the monkey mind while realizing that the highs, lows, and transitions in between are all part of the glorious process.

Having a mindfulness practice helps you feel better in general: less rushed, more calm, more awake, and aware of others. You will be resilient and less afraid in the face of obstacles. ANT thoughts will come and go quickly. The road toward your happy rat park will be paved with more acceptance, gratitude, and the ability to savor everything.

It will also become clear that enlightenment is fleeting. It comes and goes, usually in direct proportion to your personal practice.

A practice encompasses all of living, learning, loving, ego, excitement, work, hedonism, boredom, everything you do, think and experience. It is about actually finding your unique balance, rather than holding something close to balance some of the time.

Sometimes you have to give in to desires. And sometimes practicing restraint will better serve a peaceful empowered mind. Emotions are our guide. It has been said that knowledge is power. In this context emotional self-knowledge delivers the power to know when to attack life, or step back, savor, retune, relax and refocus. When in or even near balance, the meaning of life will simply become living.

~~~

Behavioral psychologists often say we have a happiness *"set-point,"* a baseline to which we return, no matter what happens or how situations change. While there is some truth in this, it seems that the attitude baseline rises with self-awareness. Making policies and practicing mindfulness tools raises the bar with a foundation of clarity and confidence.

It's like Abraham Lincoln said, "*Most folks are about as happy as they make up their minds to be.*" Happiness is an inside job. Thoughts are not perfect and could never be; that's not reality. But with a little effort, the mind can become more accepting of self and others, better at setting realistic expectations, more equipped everyday to responsibly spot and fill needs.

We are all a work in a forever, ongoing process, doing our best to shape and share the park. Get used to having to find ways to express yourself, contribute, and make life meaningful. Stop and say: if it is to be it is up to me. Once you take full responsibility to maximize living in all stages of life, good things happen.

~~~

Here are a few ideas for maximal living:

1. Dream just beyond (perceived) limits. What does the next versions of you (2.0, 3.0, 4.0) look like? What's missing? What do you have to offer? Picture your win-list and personal park as a magnet pulling toward being that person.

2. Prepare to get lucky. It's been said that luck happens when preparedness meets opportunity. Going to school, the gym, a support group, etc. can be destinations and stepping-stones. Planning is the process of preparing now for that which will support the future.

3. Other people are the mirrors through which we see ourselves. By reaching out, connecting, and supporting their dreams, you open the channel to have yours manifest.

4. Predictability is comforting. Uncertainty is exhilarating. Take chances. Go with the flow. Stay open to people, projects, and activities that pull you in, even if they are not part of your conscious plan. Remember, with quantum awareness, there are many possible futures available. Allow destiny to happen.

5. Keep a win-list journal. Do more things that make the inner-fan happy. Start building a Ulysses Contract for each of the five policy pillars. Have fun.

Happiness lies in the hunt for connection, purpose, interests, and service. This pleasure of pursuit along with silent savoring leads to finding your flow. Try art, music, business, creative hobbies, sports; any passion can be a launching pad.

Schedule unscheduled time with permission to explore interests and see what happens. Share your talents and contribute. It's up to you to find ways to enjoy living.

Our modern world brings so many distractions that it's easy to forget that we each have to make life meaningful. This must be a priority to feel fulfilled. In other words, chase your dreams or be haunted by them.

For each of the five pillars, you have purpose, passion, and reason for getting out of bed. It doesn't have to be grand, but it will never be trivial. It doesn't have to be hard, but it won't always be easy. Policies help keep thoughts and actions in alignment with purpose. Becoming self-aware can always be traced back to trusting and acting on hunches. Finding and funding your win-list is as simple as asking. If you ask, listen, learn, and live; your inner-fan will guide you.

Wisewords: *"Do what you can where you are with what you've got."* ~Theodore 'Teddy' Roosevelt

≈ Change Agent

Zoom out. Take a deep breath. Look at this beautiful world we live in. This is an exciting time to be alive. Never before have there been so many options and opportunities to live fully, connect, support, enjoy, learn, and play. This is also an urgent time with many challenges threatening society. We are at a crossroads.

Governments have risen and fallen, wars continue to be fought, companies come and go. Our lives are built on the backs of those that came before. Collective choices now will affect those that come after. As populations, government, business, media, religious and social structures have grown in size and complexity, it has become impossible for bureaucrats to manage it all effectively.

In an example, the US Government Accounting Office reported that one agency spent $12 million promoting the consumption of cheese, while another agency spent $6.5 million telling people not to eat cheese. This is ridiculous. The system is too big and complex to legislate or regulate into working responsibly.

Just as we can change the air in our lungs with each breath, we can change our world; from the inside out. When each individual takes responsibility for themselves and their universe of influence, our world will know peaceful progress.

~~~

Imagine that aliens have landed in every city on every continent and are walking down every street, looking for people to eat. Do you think you could come together with friends and foes alike to fight them off? I have news for you: the aliens are here. They show up as self-centeredness, corruption, negligence, greed, and indifference.

You, the individual, share goals and common consciousness with everyone. We all come from the same spark and are connected. Our differences are not all that different. We all want the same things. Self-improvement cannot take place in isolation. By taking care of ourselves, we take care of each other.

The pursuit of wealth and economic growth at all costs has opened doors to commerce, but has missed serving some of society's important needs. Historically, real progress only happens once there is a critical need, usually at the 11th hour.

Even then, politics, protectionism, lawyers, greed, media spin, groupthink, and inertia make smart change painfully slow.

Corporate profits should not define social progress. We are better than this. Economic stress, governmental gridlock, depression, medical costs, social isolation, housing challenges, traffic, terrorism, gun violence, bureaucracy, global warming, human trafficking, hunger, and a thousand other disturbing realities signal that some things need to change.

Let's get real about acknowledging the quirks of human nature, politics, capitalism, and globalism, then get busy living personal policies that pave the path toward sustainable public progress. The big idea is that as people grow from within, governmental, institutional, and social structures will follow. It starts with you.

As a possibility advocate, you become a change agent, an impartial servant of dreamers everywhere. Transcend limitations, both internally and externally by modeling acceptable behaviors, and rejecting unacceptable ones. You defend and encourage your own dreams, as well as the dreams, hopes, and needs of others. The possibility advocate uncovers reasons why success is possible, why ideas will work, then demonstrates both subtle and bold action.

There are plenty of organizations in need of enlightened participation and leadership. As more people remember that we are the soul of all institutions, things will change. History is not written and destiny is not set. As we participate in the re-creation of ourselves we must remember that we are also re-creating our world.

We all have ideas of the way things *"should"* be. Sometime we trust our instincts and take action. Too often we don't. The excuses are all quite logical and real: not enough, time, money, desire, influence, or connections. These *"what's in it for me?"* rationalizations keep us trapped in a rat maze chasing stale cheese. Winners in the rat race are rewarded with a rat hell.

Break free. Break the ties that bind. Tune instinct to intention. Get off the couch. Open up to the future. Now is the time to remember the true-you, accept your role, set the example, connect, and become a change agent.

Wisewords: *"You say you want a revolution? We all want to change the world."*
~ The Beatles

≈ Carrots

We have all heard the saying about the carrot at the end of the stick - the rewards that pull us through challenges. The funny thing about carrots is that although they fill you up for a bit, you are soon hungry again. You have to keep eating them. That's life. You have to keep practicing forever. And that's OK.

This book is my way of sharing a very simple message of hope and understanding. By understanding how the mind defines reality, hope is found where the pursuit of meaningful goals is balanced with enjoying life.

All of us are wizards in training, born with the ability to shape reality. With a little bit of guidance and practice we can do amazing things. Personal growth feels good, creates momentum, and makes one hungry for more, leading to the success habit. Every day, new knowledge reminds us to stay humble; knowing we can't know it all, but can find what we need by asking.

I'm certain that as soon as this manuscript is sent to the printer, new ideas will present themselves, opening doors to new chapters and new policies. It's okay. Perfection is an illusion and enemy of the good. Even imperfect people deserve to be happy. The process of progress is all that matters.

The good life is about keeping it real, feeding the inner-fan, and simply doing your best. You may find ideas and direction in books, tapes, or videos; but it's not about the book, the tape, or the video. It's about you. The things you do, the way you are day in and day out define a personal path.

We use words as the currency of ideas. We earn and spend them freely, thinking we are expressing reality. But trying to define reality is impossible. True meaning is about walking the talk in thoughts, practice, and behavior. In the end, books stay on the shelf while you leave a legacy of actions. Stay hungry and be interesting by accepting everything gratefully. Expect the best. Get what you need while helping others do the same. There aren't always easy answers to our complicated questions; but there are always answers. Keep questioning.

Wisewords: *"What lies behind us and what lies before us are tiny matters compared to what lies within us."* ~Ralph Waldo Emerson

Appendix: Ulysses Contract & the Future You

There is a difference between wanting to upgrade the life experience and actually making progress. This is one aspect of human nature we all face. Even though we are wired to take care of ourselves, picking priorities and making changes can feel difficult or complicated. Inside we often know we want some things to change, but don't always know the steps to get there.

To understand why, step back and see yourself as two different people: the *"now you,"* and the *"future you."* The *"now you"* can dream up all sorts of goals. It is fun and exciting to think about how great it will be to lose weight, change careers, change a habit, make new friends, find love or whatever you think you need. It's easy to set goals even when we know there will be challenges.

But it is the *"future you"* who will face the challenges. Without self-awareness and a plan, the *"future you"* is weak, distracted, sub-conscious, focused on wants, guided by dusty old beliefs, and stuck in tired routines. The *"future you"* can be an arrogant pain in the ass.

If you aren't alert to the benefits of change on an intellectual and emotional level, impulse takes over. Without preparation, most of us will pick the path of least resistance and make poor choices in the moments that matter.

When temptation strikes and the bratty ego takes over, good intentions go out the window. A piece of pie, a drink, less study, more phone/Internet/video game/TV, credit card purchase, cigarette - any quick fix can sound good in the moment. Over time, failure brings frustration, so we quit trying to change.

Ulysses Contract (UC) mindfulness map gives the rational, conscious, *"now"* you a way to guide the impulsive *"future"* you into making smart choices that stick naturally. This tool delivers a reliable technique to beat the cycle of defeat then builds a pattern of progress.

It works by clearly painting a picture of the *"future you,"* charging it with emotion, navigating past obstacles, and setting consequences if you go off course. You can call this rigging the game, the law of attraction, trusting the process, or just old-fashioned wise livin'. Success breeds confidence; it gets easier all the time to live as the true-you.

Ask yourself where you will be at this time next year. Without a plan, the odds are you'll be near where you are at, just a little older. Life passes by faster than you could ever imagine. Ulysses Contracts put the universe to work by keeping you movin' & groovin'. They can be used alongside any religion, personal growth program, or spiritual path to supercharge conscious evolution. By creating these, you are asking important questions, taking action on needs, rewiring beliefs, building energy, feeding faith, and investing in yourself as a force of nature.

UCs are a place to unite and focus the power from as many sources as necessary to build up enough positive pressure to expand your reality zone. These are pacts you make with yourself to map a course forward while preparing for the challenges that are sure to come.

Just wanting change is not enough, though. The desire has to be authentic and in alignment with the true-you. Once you have needs and priorities clear, amazing things start to happen. Your thoughts, words, and actions might even surprise you!

Why Ulysses? Ulysses, also known as Odysseus (his name in the original Greek version), was the subject of Homer's epic poem, *The Odyssey*. Renowned for his resourcefulness, Ulysses is remembered for the Trojan Horse and his brilliant plan to savor then escape from the Sirens.

The Sirens were dangerous creatures, aquatic seductresses who lured sailors with songs of enchantment to shipwreck off the rocky coast of their island. In Book VII of The Odyssey, the goddess Circe gives Ulysses the option to hear the beautiful but deadly Sirens. He wanted to hear their song but knew that doing so would render him incapable of rational thought, leading to destruction. Ulysses wanted to hear the song and survive.

To do this, he had his men tie him to the ship's mast, then put wax in their ears so they could row but not hear. He ordered them not to change course under any circumstances and to put their swords upon him should he break free of his bonds.

Upon hearing the Sirens' song, Ulysses was driven temporarily insane and struggled with all of his might to break free. He begged his crew to release him. With every stroke, the oarsmen helped Ulysses to move past temptation. The pact held. After having rowed beyond the danger zone, crewmembers removed the wax and freed a grateful Ulysses.

Ulysses rigged the game for success by knowing his limits, then creating a plan to work within them. The plan he made to row past the sirens is the same design for contracts we can make with ourselves to get what we need while rowing past unhealthy thoughts or destructive temptations. Just as with Ulysses, we will all face challenges that can be solved by realizing that there are often hooks inside the tempting bait that floats by. Don't take that bait.

UCs help build up enough awareness to stay true to your higher self when the bratty "*future you*" attempts to take over. It works by blending intention and strategy with wisdom. Once you realize how great it feels to stop biting into hooked bait the temptation to do so fades. This awareness sharpens the ability to spot tasty hook-free bait and the confidence to grab it.

~~~

Some things in life are easier to change than others. Short-term goals can happen effortlessly when the reward is close at hand and clearly defined. Changing long-

148

term beliefs, patterns, addictions, etc., is tougher, but can be done. Ulysses showed us the way.

The power of the Ulysses Contract comes from focusing on the new and improved win-list version of yourself, then steadily moving in the right direction. They help us to keep rowing, even when the big picture and the rewards seem fuzzy or far away.

Making Ulysses Contracts is about confirming a date with your future self. It is amazing how fast desire, clear intention, visualization, and practice will rewire beliefs about what is possible. This tool unites the forces of change in a compact, tidy format designed to help resist the siren song of the inner-critic.

Wisewords: *"Nothing is impossible, the word itself says 'I'm possible'!"* ~Audrey Hepburn

Getting Started Making Contracts

Ulysses Contracts work on goals that we know we need and know we're capable of reaching, but just can't focus our energy on or don't know the exact steps to take. Things like better diet, less media, saving money, staying connected with friends, having adventures, more fun, finding a better job, a sweetheart, losing weight, getting fit, or changing drugs/drinking/smoking patterns are all life upgrades that you deserve. Make a contract for anything you need.

Think of this process like water building up behind a dam. The dam is the limiting belief and the behavior you want to change. The UC represents the water wanting to flow. As your conscious mind fills in your plan, the subconscious adds emotional pressure to create the change.

Sometimes the water breaks through and the new beliefs take hold quickly. Sometimes the water will build up and stagnate due to resistance from the ego. Usually, the water just trickles through slowly, building momentum, clearing your path.

Often there is a desire for change but the absence of a strategy or workable plan keeps us stuck in old patterns. Ulysses Contracts deliver solutions by unlocking dependable personal policies. They work if you believe that the BeSMART goals you pick are in alignment with the true-you. This method focuses intentional energy on the changes we want and need to make. The act of creating a contract starts the process and feels good.

One way to approach this activity is to make an ongoing contract for each of the five policy pillars. Or pick just one area to focus on. Add inspiration, information, insight, and examples as they reveal themselves to you. Building these agreements develops vigilance in spotting ways to live your win-list.

~~~

Ask the right questions. Point yourself in the right direction, invest some energy, and nature will do the rest. Sometimes, just considering whether to make a UC is enough to trigger change. Don't let ego trick you into thinking you got it though. Empower the future you by filling in details, policies and emotions. Mark the start date but don't sign it. Take it seriously. After all, why would you want to break a contract with yourself?

Sometimes a UC will linger unsigned when all of a sudden you realize that what you were hoping for has become to reality. This happens all the time. It is a sign of authentic change that just needed a little push. In this case, pull out your original contract, add some detail and feeling about what's working, sign it, put it away, and revisit it occasionally.

For other things, it will take some time to build up energy to actually make the changes stick. It depends on how ready you are to push through tired old routines. In these cases, keep adding detail and stay mindful for insight on ways to move closer to yourself. Add notes to build up pressure. When you feel ready, sign it, reward yourself with a big thank you and a sigh of relief, then get ready for critic ego to speak. But as a policy expert, you already know that and will be ready with firm responses.

~~~

Pull completed contracts and ones in progress out to add strategic detail and emotion regularly. Zero in on the beliefs that you are trying to change and find policies that support the upgrade. Look for groups, information, and activities that support your vision of success. Capture observations and insight on what's working and feels right. Keep rewarding success. Getting clear on true desires begins to make them a reality.

There is a lot of pressure and expectation around status, looks, relationships, work, and more in modern life. There will be challenges. We are not machines meant to constantly grind away, strive, push.... It's normal to go a little mad at times. Staying sane demands that you must be ready to declare breakdowns, let off pressure, regroup, and move on. UCs are part of smart breakdowns that you can use to navigate transitions graciously.

Just as bodies need a break everyday, the mind needs a way to step back, relax, and refocus. Coping mechanisms like shopping, drugs, food, alcohol, and sex take the mind off the stressors, but never very far away. Using a UC to declare a smart breakdown grants permission to say *"X, Y, or Z isn't working and I need to make some changes."* Raising the white flag of surrender books a ticket on the journey to the true-you. This may take a minute or a month, but denying the needs never works. Once you admit limits and embrace change you will come back refreshed and ready for more.

The old, deep-seated stories and responses played for decades with parents, friends, siblings, and the opposite sex often run unconsciously. The beliefs on self-worth and expectations of others take time to change. Don't beat yourself up; just keep clearing a path closer to a natural groove. Be gentle and allow time to re-imagine, recreate, and reclaim the true-you. When you do make it through the storm relax and celebrate; you will be stronger and better equipped to do it next time.

Wisewords: *"If your ship doesn't come in, swim out to it!"* ~Jonathan Winters

> Activity: Make a Ulysses Contract

This is where the rubber hits the road. Use your rational *"now"* mind to steer subconscious future thoughts. Design an approach that will bring change at a manageable pace. Build in a series of rewards that will pull you forward. Build in exits that allow you to take the pressure off. Realize that there will be times when the bratty ego critic will scream what an idiot you are for trying to make this change. Have a firm response ready. Remember, it's about progress, not perfection.

Sometimes, just creating and signing a contract will get you clear on your intentions and get pointed in the right direction. Other times, it will take a little longer. This approach works on the conscious and subconscious level to bring expectations into alignment with reality.

Once you start upgrading the B.OS, change will start happening in subtle and often invisible ways. With consistency of purpose, the new you will emerge as the true-you - more alert, aware, and awake to joy and purpose. It took a long time to define your present-self. Allow your inner-fan the time to re-imagine and recreate your future. With Ulysses on your side, someday is today.

Here is a step-by-step guide to putting a Ulysses Contract to work. Use a journal to fill in details to the following sections. Or download the Ulysses Contract PDF at PolicyPillars.com under Toolbox, then start building your first contract.

Date: Note the current date.

Pillar • Most goals cross two, three, or even all five pillars. Choose one as the primary category this contract fills taking mental note of the related pillars.

BeSMART goal • These are Believable, Emotionally charged, Specific, Measurable, Actionable, Realistic and Timely. Keep in mind that most goals change shape as you progress toward them. See section: BeSMART goals.

Priorities & Vision • Describe why this goal is important to you. Focus on the deeper emotional feeling that pulls toward wanting change in this direction. List the benefits and how moving forward will feel. Paint a picture of your personal park and win-list success. What does it feel like, who will share it, what could it lead to?

Stories, Beliefs, Fears & Obstacles • What is holding progress back? What blind spots need awareness and planning to overcome? What stories do you tell yourself and others? What beliefs might be in the way? What fears control behavior? How can they be changed?

Be honest with yourself about the challenges you know will come up. Look for obstacles in advance to spot where plans might break down. What techniques and strategies will be used to fulfill this contract? What wise policies have worked for others? Before long, desires will become reflexes and former obstacles will become reminders of the power to change. See chapter: Master of the Universe

Personal Policies • What maxims, quotes, affirmations, wise counsel, techniques, or strategies can you adopt to guide your path? What priorities will harness and focus emotional energy? See sections: Beyond Goals to Policy, Making Policy Personal, Develop Your Personal Policies, and Mind Your Mantra.

How to Rig The Game for Success • This section is about how to get the conscious mind to guide subconscious thoughts. Ask how to help the *"now you"* guide the *"future you"* you into making smart choices. Are you leveraging strengths? Being realistic with yourself about expectations? Know the limits and have a strategy to work within them. Frame your strategy through a lens of how good accomplishing your goal is going to make you feel. Once you become deeply invested in wanting the best life possible, it becomes possible.

Observations • Fill this section in as you go to build up information, insight, and energy. Add detail, feelings, observations, and examples of what is working. What isn't working? Why? What are the consequences of not making your best effort?

This is the eyes, ears, and heart of the Ulysses Contract. It is about gathering energy from the past, present and future to build up enough momentum so that the change you want becomes a natural extension of everything happening. It's a place to capture thoughts, ideas, and experiences that together will help define policies you can trust, believe in, and lean on.

Consequences: UCs are designed to help personal growth happen naturally, but sometimes setting consequences for not reaching goals can be a powerful motivator. Connecting the consequences to people builds a strong sense of accountability. Consequences and peer pressure work. Rig the game by playing human nature off itself. Put some skin in the game by making it real with whatever will motivate you to stay the course.

Set any type of consequence that will have meaning to you. It may be a financial payment to a person or charity. Time consequences such as commitment to volunteering or going back to school to learn more if you cannot accomplish the contract. Maybe simply wanting to avoid regrets will be enough. Make accountability real by setting deadlines, posting on social media, and having any money at stake held by a third-party. Meet regularly with the people you have made commitments to.

It is also smart to allow some flexibility in consequences. Research shows that allowing cheat days on diets and other goals helps let some steam off to keep from falling off the wagon. Finding that perfect balance of consequences that have meaning while allowing for the hedonic deviations needed by human nature is the trick.

Consequences can be retroactive. Odds are, you have already put a good deal of time or energy into some of your bigger goals. You can pull energy from those investments. Many years after starting this book, I was ready to give up. I made a contract to do my best to pull it together. I drew energy from the fear of losing all the time and money invested up to that point. That was a strong motivator, but not quite enough. Knowing I needed help, I hired a book coach who wanted $500 up front. Investments from the past along with new investment pushed the scale to tip and I got back to work. Don't lose heart if you have to spend time and money or pay out on some consequences to get ahead; consider it an investment in the future you.

★ **Expectations** • How do you think this will go? Be willing to rewrite stories about lovability, self-worth, options, and abilities. Are you ready to rewrite your stories? Ask yourself what your win-list version of this looks and feels like.

Reward • How and when will you recognize and reward yourself? Rig the game by hanging a carrot or two just out of reach. As you reach milestones, take credit, and treat yourself to a play, music event, dinner out, or massage. Make it an experience you really want or something related to the original goal. Supercharge it with accountability by picking something you can share with someone, then let them know.

Inspiration • Who are the people who inspire you to succeed? Who has accomplished similar things and can be a source of energy for you? What books, seminars, speakers, documentaries, shows, etc., have wisdom you can put to work? Who can you connect with that might be of help?

Successes and New Beliefs • This section is a ton of fun. As you navigate the process of upgrading mental software, instances of insight and understanding will begin to happen more and more often. Make note and enjoy.

Notes & Lessons Learned on this path • This is where to bring it all together in the context of your unique life. Have you done your best? Can you check this off your win-list? What do the next steps look like? Odd are you will realize that solving one thing only leads to the next thing, and that it's awesome being empowered while making progress!

Help somebody else • How can you pay it forward by helping someone else? How to best use what you have learned? The process of teaching others cements the wisdom in your own mind.

Doodles • Pictures are the symbolic language of the mind and can be worth a thousand words. Draw images that you associate with the massive pleasure this contract promises.

As you are ready, add your signature and date.

_____ _____

Note: This is a fluid technique updated occasionally.
Find the latest Ulysses Contract version PDF download at the PPI web site.

Wisewords: *"I have enjoyed life a lot more by saying 'yes' than by sayings 'no.'"*
~Richard Branson

Acknowledgements

I gratefully thank all my supporters and collaborators, the people who helped make these words meaningful. My parents, who pushed for education while putting up with my rebellious nature. My Sacramento crew, who taught me how to live, then urged me to write something down. Kudos goes to early reviewers, Amberly Fineralli and Laura Davis (lauradavis.net), who guided and encouraged this project. Agatha Golonkiewicz Malina who "*got it*," and then designed the perfect logo out of nothing but an idea on a lunch napkin doodle. Ms. Angelica Valentine for asking hard questions in a loving way. My pals Blaze for patiently listening as I worked out thoughts on our travels (renegadejuggling.com) and Kevin *'Buzz'* for creative support. Good friends Dana and Sarah for ongoing support, feedback, and encouragement. Jenifer Novak-Landers for inspiration and encouragement. Taoist master Carl Abbott for reminding me that free will may not exist, but it's still worth trying (centao.org). My editor extraordinaire Claudia Graziano who stepped up to the challenge helping to distill 160,000 rambling words into a readable 40,000. My eleventh-hour readers Lynda, Harllee, Wendy, Cormac and Patricia, whose eagle eyes spotted unruly content, commas, and coherence. Additional appreciation goes out to Alicia Scholer for her amazing proofreaders deep cleaning. My cat Jack (RIP) =^..^= who tirelessly sat by and often on my work. Radio KZSC the Great 88 for some long sweet late night jams to write by. And to all the beautiful people who made time to listen and share, thank you.

Did you enjoy this book? If so, please leave a review with your favorite bookseller.

About the author

Jeff Hotchkiss MBA, is a possibility advocate and rebel with a cause to promote mindfulness as a path to empowerment. He has been an executive with Apple Computer, founder of Olivus^{TM} teas, and publishing entrepreneur. Armed with endless curiosity, he has studied psychology, philosophy, physics, spirituality, and more in search of modern answers to the timeless questions. Based in Northern California, he coaches, speaks and leads workshops on practical mindfulness.

Wisewords: *Aspire to inspire before you expire!"* ~Eugene Bell Jr.

Notes:

Printed by BoD™in Norderstedt, Germany